PRAYING
FOR A
MIRACLE:

A Mother's Story of Tragedy, Hope and Triumph

by

Gilda T. D'Agostino

With Best Wishes

Gilda T D'Agostino

Ambassador Books, Inc.
Worcester • Massachusetts

Library of Congress Cataloging-in-Publication Data

D'Agostino, Gilda T., 1926-
   Praying for a miracle : a mother's story of tragedy, hope, and triumph / by
Gilda T. D'Agostino.
         .
      p. cm.
   ISBN 1-929039-29-8 (pbk.)
   1. D'Agostino, Richard J.--Health. 2. Quadriplegics--Massachusetts Biography.
3. Spinal cord--Wounds and injuries--Patients--Massachusetts--Biography. 4.
Spinal cord--Wounds and injuries--Patients--Rehabilitation. I. Title.

   RC406.Q33D34 2005
   362.197'482044'092--dc22

                                    2005023438

Published in the United States by Ambassador Books, Inc.
91 Prescott Street, Worcester, Massachusetts 01605
(800) 577-0909

Printed in the United States of America.

For current information about all titles from Ambassador Books, Inc.,
visit our website at: www.ambassadorbooks.com.

DEDICATION

To my husband Tony J. D'Agostino —

Without his patience, time and compassion, our son's life would not be so successful and free of financial burdens. Most important, however, has been his emotional support. His constant concern for Rick's safety and comfort allayed my always present anxiety.

ACKNOWLEDGEMENTS

The author would like to thank all those who helped with this book: Cecile Carroll of Paxton who led me to Ambassador Books and Elizabeth Deese for the several hours spent copy editing at her home in Holden.

I wish to especially thank Gerry Goggins and Jennifer Conlan, my editors, for their kindness, patience and knowledge and for spending countless hours editing each chapter. Their genuine interest in producing this book was greatly appreciated. The book could not have been done without their assistance. I shall forever be grateful to them.

FOREWORD

This is the story of how a severe accident forever changed the life of my son and the lives of our family members. It is my hope that it will give others who must face severe disabilities the courage to persevere and the knowledge that the human spirit can be indomitable even in the worst of circumstances.

This is the story of Rick, my middle child, who has spent more than three decades as a quadriplegic, but it is told through the eyes of his mother. It is the account of how my family and I coped with our tragedy, and how my son triumphed over his physical handicaps.

Without the use of both hands and both legs Rick has accomplished the seemingly impossible. His attitude, courage, determination and faith in God have made him a truly unique individual. He is a successful businessman who works out of his home selling his inventions which make the lives of other disabled people richer and easier.

In June of 1973, Richard J. D'Agostino graduated from St. John's High School in Shrewsbury, Massachusetts. One month after graduation, his life changed drastically. His plan for a career as an electrician came to an abrupt end when he dove into a city swimming pool where he was working as a lifeguard. The impact severed his spinal cord, leaving him paralyzed from the neck down and with very limited use of his arms. His goal at that time was focused on learning to live a new life as a quadriplegic. Thanks to strong family support and many loving and caring friends, Rick found strength from within and without to master many routine activities.

Rick received the Kopka Memorial Award for demonstrating the courage, perseverance and character to overcome physical disability and to deal with adversity.

Rick was the first person in a wheelchair to attend Cape Cod Community College. Rick and the college staff overcame many obstacles and his experience created many positive changes for students with disabilities at the college. After graduation in 1981, he remained at the college as a computer lab attendant, a position he held for more than twenty years. He is highly regarded for his patience while helping needy students.

Though he learned to drive his own custom, handicapped-equipped van, he encountered some problems operating the vehicle. Setting his mind to the task, he worked to solve them. He built a wireless remote to open the doors and to operate the van's lift. He also built a custom steering device for safety. This is typical of what he has accomplished throughout his more than three decades of being disabled, and it illustrates how he has helped himself and assisted others who have found themselves in a similar condition.

In 1985, Rick invented the Electric Leg Bag Emptier and started his own business, R. D. Equipment, Inc. He created one emptier for a standard electric wheelchair, another for a battery controlled wheelchair and a third with a sip and puff switch for those who use their mouths to operate the chair.

In 1991, Rick designed and built his post and beam home in West Barnstable, Massachusetts. He loves to travel, but he encountered problems with bathroom access in many hotels. Rick holds a patent on the Tub Slide Shower Chair, which allows quadriplegics complete access to any bathroom. This invention is the latest addition to his company's product line. R. D. Equipment has been able to help disabled people throughout the world, thanks also to Rick's father who has provided his able hands to accomplish these rewarding tasks.

I have been encouraged to write this book by many of Rick's friends. I am grateful for their encouragement.

CHAPTER ONE

THE GRADUATION

The bitter cold and stormy weather had become a memory. A chilly spring was turning toward a glorious New England summer. Flowers and shrubs were in bloom, showing off their brilliant sunny colors of orange, pink and red. The buds on the trees had exploded into leaves. The sky was blue, the day was sunny, and life was good. It was graduation time—and it was time for a family party.

It was 1973 and my son Rick was seventeen and had just graduated from St. John's High School in Shrewsbury, Massachusetts. It was a special milestone for Rick and for our entire family. Rick had never liked school. Although he did well in mathematics and science, he had a difficult time with reading, spelling and writing. His happiest time in school was when he played on the football team and attended proms with his girlfriend.

Rick is my middle child. He has an older brother, Bob, and a younger sister, Gina. He is six feet tall with sandy colored curly hair, light brown eyes and a stocky build—somewhat unusual for an Italian. His brother and sister both have dark skin and hair and are slimmer than he.

Tony, my husband, and I came from large Italian families. I am the ninth child of twelve and Tony is the fifth child of eight, so there is a lot of family. Rick's aunts, uncles and cousins number about sixty-five and they all were invited to Rick's graduation party. The party was planned two weeks after graduation because Rick was convalescing from minor knee surgery and was using crutches.

The day was perfect—beautiful, mild, sunny and calm. As I looked over our big backyard, it seemed like the perfect spot for a family celebration. The grounds were simply maintained with a plush lawn and some flowering bushes. The patio was an ideal place for setting up large tables. My husband is always a great help in all this preparation. He staples white paper to the buffet tables, rents chairs for our guests, and arranges cold drinks packed in ice. Sometimes when rain threatens we rent a tent that Tony puts up without difficulty, but on this day, there was no need for a tent.

I could not have been happier. I enjoy entertaining and cooking. Coming from a large family, there is always a party going on be it a christening, birthday, bridal shower, wedding or anniversary. And I enjoyed every minute of preparing for Rick's party. The menu consisted of my family's favorite foods: Italian meatballs and sausage, ziti, macaroni with sauce, eggplant parmigiana, potato salad, cold cuts and lots of Italian bread, assorted fruits, and tossed salad. For dessert there was an assortment of goodies plus a large sheet cake that had written on it "Congratulations Rick."

As the guests arrived in the late afternoon, Rick greeted them with his contagious smile and firm hand shakes for the men and big kisses for his aunts. His maternal grandmother arrived a bit late. She used a cane because of two arthritic hips that caused her to hobble as she came across the patio. She always dressed meticulously. Her hair was curled, and she sported her favorite jewelry. She bore twelve children, outlived her husband by many years, and was as bright as any fifty-year-old. When you kissed her, she smelled like Johnson's baby powder. She always spoke words of wisdom and always had a word of encouragement. "If someone else can do it, you can also" or "If you like what you're doing, you will do it well," she would say. She received a special hug and kiss from Rick.

Rick was having a great time. Most guests presented him with a monetary gift, which naturally pleased him. Tony and I gave him a gift that made his eyes widen. It was a large tool chest with an assortment of tools.

"Boy, now I can have my own tools and not have to borrow my Dad's," he said when he opened the package.

"And I won't be looking for my tools anymore," his father responded.

Naturally, during the course of the party, Rick was asked over and over about his future plans.

Rick's answer was short and to the point.

"I don't like school, so I'm not going to college."

His short-term plan was to work as a lifeguard at a city pool for the summer. He had taken an extension course in lifeguarding given by the American Red Cross to qualify as a lifeguard and therefore was well prepared. He planned to start the job as soon as the doctor gave him the "O.K." to put away the crutches.

Rick was also forming a long-term plan. His cousin, Ray Duquette owned a successful electrical contracting business.

Rick planned to speak to him about eventually enrolling in a technical school to learn the business.

Rick needed the break from studying. The twelve long years of schooling were not easy for him. When he was in kindergarten, we had a conference with his teacher. She praised his ability in distinguishing shapes and sizes and felt he was ready to read. We were happy to hear he was doing well. We read to our children every night at bedtime and if one of us tried to skip a page to hurry things along, eagle-eye Rick would be there to catch us. He would pick it up immediately.

By the time he got into fourth grade it became evident that his reading ability was questionable. In fact he could not read. I began to think that there must be something wrong with his brain. I even made an appointment with a psychiatrist who did a brain test or an EEG. He determined that everything was normal. The frustration continued. Another conference was held with his teacher that led us to have his eyes examined. The eye doctor prescribed mild reading glasses, probably unnecessary, that Rick used while in school. It pleased his teacher but his reading did not improve. I wanted the school administrators to hold him back for a year, in hopes it would help him but they did not agree. They said his I.Q. was above normal. As a last resort Tony and I decided to talk to a child psychologist. At our visit with the specialist we talked about our son, his activities, his lack of interest in school and his inability to read and spell. The psychologist could easily sense how disturbed, frustrated and concerned we were. My other children were average students without any problems in school, but Rick was different in many ways.

"Does your son have lots of friends?" the psychologist asked.

"Yes, he is with friends all the time," we said.

"Does he play hard?"

"Yes, he's outdoors all day, fishing, swimming, biking and going all the time."

"Then don't worry so much about him, he's going to be all right," the doctor said. We left the office feeling somewhat better.

When Rick was about ten years old, his cousin Dick Pickett, a devoted elementary school teacher, noticed my son's manual ability and the successful things he had accomplished. We had spoken with Dick several times about Rick's school problems. Rick had a good vocabulary and expressed himself well. He was alert to everything around him and especially anything technical. He could listen to a car engine and could tell if it was running well or in need of a tune-up.

Dick was attending courses at the University of Connecticut working toward his Master's Degree in education. The course he was taking was Diagnostic Reading Disabilities. Dick could see Rick was a brilliant child. As a matter of fact, he asked us permission to use Rick as the subject of a thesis he was working on for his master's degree.

Rick was a perfect candidate for the testing that was required for part of the course. Dick arrived one day with a pencil and paper and tested Rick for about one hour. He had Rick do a reading inventory, starting from lower grade levels and working up to the present grade level. Rick did well. The results of the test showed Rick did not have a learning disability or dyslexia. Rick was too mechanically inclined to have a deep interest in the academic curriculum which school was presenting and he showed lack of motivation. Dick was pleased with the results.

During school vacation, when Rick was in his early teens, we sent him to 4H Camp in Spencer for two weeks. He enjoyed it greatly. His friend, Andy Spahr, went with him and they both practically ran the whole show. They liked swimming, horseback riding, playing games, campfires and singing.

Rick and Andy enjoyed outdoor fun. Many times they could be found at a small brook not far from our home catching frogs. They proceeded to dissect the legs, make a fire outdoors, borrow flour, butter and my frying pan and have the delicacy of fried frog legs.

Tony had a method of calling our children home. He would place two fingers in his mouth and give a shrill whistle that could be heard throughout the neighborhood. One time he tried to call Rick home for a dentist appointment. Rick was too far way to hear it, so Tony had to go to the brook where the boys were catching frogs to get him. Tony's arrival scared a large frog to safety—away from the long stick my son was eagerly wielding.

"Now look what you did, Dad, you scared that big frog away."

"Come on, Rick, you're going to be late for your appointment."

As Rick was hurrying home, a few of the frog legs that he had placed in his pocket fell out, much to his disappointment.

During his early teens, he spent many summer days swimming in Indian Lake, a short distance from our home, with his gang of friends. One of his friends had a home on the lake and his mother would give the boys lunch. Often he spent most of the day there. He became a very strong swimmer. Years later, he would often look back and say what a wonderful childhood he had.

The graduation party was highly successful. It proceeded without a hitch. Everyone left in good spirits. Tony and I, as usual, were faced with enough food to last us the whole coming week.

Rick was happy. He had had a great time. School was finally over, and the future seemed very bright indeed.

CHAPTER TWO

THE ACCIDENT

It was July sixteenth. My husband was in Worcester working part-time at my brother's paving contracting company, Ricciardi's Construction Company. I was on the Cape with my fourteen-year-old daughter, Gina enjoying the beautiful summer day. My boys were in Worcester. Bob worked as a lifeguard at Bell Pond, a job he had had the previous summer and Rick was at his first job after graduation working as a lifeguard at Maloney Field.

I felt relaxed and free from worries. The boys were doing well, especially Rick. He was finished with school and extremely happy about it. I was happy spending time alone with my daughter, and we were enjoying a girls' weekend. My sister-in-law, Charlotte, was visiting us on this particular day. We had lunch at the Wee Packet, a quaint little breakfast and lunch restaurant on Sea Street in Dennisport, near the beach. We all ordered the lobster roll, a favorite of anyone familiar with the restaurant.

We got back to the Cape house about two o'clock. We were

in very good moods. It was a beautiful day, and we had just finished a terrific lunch. We were laughing and joking with each other when the phone rang.

It was my brother, Vincent, calling from Worcester.

"You've got to come home right away. Rick's at City Hospital. He's been badly injured."

The phone call was the beginning of the worst day our lives. It was a day that would change us forever.

My brother was a lieutenant on the Worcester Fire Department, and he was on duty when his company was called to the scene of an accident. When he arrived he discovered that the victim was Rick. Rick had already been given CPR, and he was in the ambulance on the way to the hospital. It was not regular procedure, but my brother asked his driver to follow the ambulance to the hospital—it was Vincent's nephew and everybody understood. The entire company pulled up at the hospital's emergency entrance. My brother jumped out of the cab and hurried in. Dr. John Bianchi, a personal friend of the family met my brother. My husband, Tony, had been called away from his construction site and was already with my son in the examining room.

"It doesn't look good," the doctor told my brother.

My brother could not stay. He slowly walked away with his head down. And the fire company returned to the fire station.

The phone call had shattered me. My heart sunk, my mind raced, and my body trembled. Blood rushed to my face and I became flushed. My arms and legs felt weak. I was in shock, but I knew that I had to collect my thoughts and find a way to get home as soon as possible.

I was in no condition to make the two-and-a-half-hour drive back to Worcester. After some phone calls, I learned from my sister-in-law, Mary, that her sister Lil had plans to leave the Cape for Worcester. I called Lil and Ray Neilson, who were happy to drive us home.

The ride home from the Cape seemed endless. The Neilson's were sensitive to my inner turmoil. There was very little talk. I was deep in thought and frightened at what I would have to face when we arrived.

How seriously was Rick hurt? Was it just a broken limb? But deep within me, I feared something far more serious.

Lil opened her purse and took out a small yellow capsule. "Take this, it will help you to calm down, it's a mild tranquilizer my doctor had prescribed," she said.

"I don't want to take anything," I said. "I'll be alright."

But Lil was insistent, and I finally gave in. As a medical professional, I knew I should not take another person's medication. In any case, the pill had no affect. I was too stressed, scared and disturbed.

When we finally arrived at the hospital, we parked at the emergency entrance and I immediately rushed to the surgical intensive care unit where Rick was. It was four o'clock, and all the medical procedures had been completed.

 Rick was lying motionless in his bed. His head was in traction, he had a tracheotomy tube inserted in his throat, an intravenous feeding tube in his arm, and a tube inserted in his penis to drain his urine. He could only move his lips and his eyes. He looked very sick. I knew immediately, without the doctors telling me, that my son had a spinal cord injury. Perhaps my lively, outgoing, active son, on the threshold of his adult life, would never walk, work on his beloved jalopy or have his own children. I felt crushed.

I was helpless, defenseless and powerless. It felt as if a hun-

dred-foot tidal wave was coming at me and I couldn't swim.
My mind became a jumble of tangled thoughts—why, how,
what for, with no answers to all of these questions. The pow-
erlessness and helplessness could not be relieved by consoling. Who could console me? My family was helpless too. How
could my husband, children or family console me when they
felt the same as I did? Even the physician could not help.
Those caring for my son felt as helpless as I knowing there is
no cure for this type of injury. With no one to console me, I
turned to God. I prayed, made novena, attended daily mass
and read spiritual passages as well as any positive readings I
could get my hands on. There was nothing to make things better. There are no words to describe this devastating injury and
what it does to the family and the individual involved. In a
split second the whole world is turned upside down.

My husband had been with Rick through all the medical
procedures. I felt bad that I had not been with Rick too, but
as I reflected on it, I thought that perhaps it was just as well.
As a nurse, I was only too aware of the pain and anxiety he
must have experienced. It would have been an emotional
black hole for me.

Our family stood at Rick's bedside. It was hard for us to
accept the reality of the situation. We were stunned. Not one
of us cried. Part of the reason was our shock and part of the
reason that we did not want Rick to see us crying. So we held
back our tears.

I kissed Rick's warm face and held his paralyzed hand. and
kept repeating, "You're going to be alright."

Rick was unable to speak with the tracheotomy tube in his
throat, but his lips kept framing the words: "I love you" and
"What did I do?"

He could not remember what had happened to him.

His first week at work had been uneventful. His dad had provided transportation to and from the pool. Rick came home all smiles. He was enjoying every minute of his new job.

The day of the accident was very hot. Rick had just finished his lunch and the pool area was quiet. He decided to take a quick dip to cool off. No one will ever know exactly what happened. We surmised that he stood at the farthest end and took a shallow dive, skimming the top of the water like a fish, something he and others had done hundreds of times. This time something terrible happened. He apparently hit the opposite end of the pool snapping his head backwards. He was unable to get out of the pool. He remained under water for a few minutes before one of the other lifeguards noticed him. They grabbed his long curly hair to pull him out of the water, performed CPR and took him to City Hospital.

When he arrived at the hospital, he was unable to move his extremities. Fortunately, on hand at the time were visiting staff physicians, Dr. Bernard Stone, neurologist, Dr. Raul Endriga, a pulmonary specialist, and Dr. John Bianchi, an orthopedic surgeon trained to treat this sort of injury. But they could do nothing to restore Rick's motion.

That was the horror of it. We had to face the possibility that our son would spend the rest of his life without the use of his arms or legs — our son who was so energetic and athletic; our son who sparkled with the joy of living. The helplessness we felt brought us to the lowest point in our lives. How were we going to cope?

When Dr. Stone arrived to check on Rick, I asked him, "What are the results of the X-rays?"

"The X-rays show a dislocation of the fifth and sixth cervical vertebrae. It's not the best injury or the worst," the doctor said.

We stayed with Rick until about ten o'clock when he was settled for the night.

And then we went back to the empty house. It was then that we hugged and cried. Bob cried. Tony cried.

I cried.

Gina, my beautiful fourteen-year-old daughter ran to her bedroom, threw herself on her bed and sobbed. She was a sophomore at a private parochial school, Marion High School in Worcester. These were supposed to be the best years of life. She was a cheerleader and a good student. At the time of the accident, she received several heart-warming notes of condolences from friends that helped her immensely, but she was hurt and sad. Like me, she cried a lot. Rick was a special brother to her, not like her older brother Bob who teased her often and made her angry. Rick and Gina were buddies. There was mutual love between them.

✤   ✤   ✤

How were we going to cope?

I asked God to help us. I asked him to give us some answers. But no answers came.

None of us had eaten but we were not hungry. We tried to get some rest, but sleep would not come. My husband and I cried in each others' arms. We cried but there was no relief. I couldn't wait for daylight so I could get back to the hospital to be with Rick.

CHAPTER THREE

THE SECOND DAY

When morning arrived, we were anxious to get to the hospital. Just looking at one another brought more tears. My husband tried to be the brave one in the group.

"We've done enough crying. Now it's time to start thinking so we can figure out how to help Rick," he said.

We quickly got ourselves ready to leave for the hospital. I wanted to get there in time to speak to the night nurse before she went off duty.

We arrived at six thirty and found Rick just as we had left him. There was no apparent improvement in his condition. We waited anxiously to see his doctor again. No one mentioned "Spinal Cord Injury" to us but I knew better.

I knew about the spinal cord and spinal cord injuries. I knew that the spinal cord is essentially a continuation of the brain. It is a tightly packed bundle of nerves that resembles a pigtail. It is three quarters of an inch thick and runs from the base of the brain down the middle of the back, ending at the waist. Its nerve fibers carry instructions from the brain to the rest of the body. The spinal cord sends signals from the body to the brain—sensations, such as pain, itching, hunger and virtually every other feeling we experience. Paralysis results when the spinal cord and its nerves are injured or affected by a neurological disease. The severity of symptoms depends on how badly the cord is damaged and at what level. The spinal cord is located within the spinal canal of the vertebral column. The vertebrae are stacked one on top of the other to form a canal. The surrounding vertebrae provide a sturdy shelter for the enclosed spinal cord.

The spinal column has five sections, seven cervical or neck, twelve thoracic or chest, five lumbar or lower back, five small sacral and a tailbone. Nerve fibers exit and enter the spinal column between the vertebrae.

When injury occurs in the spinal cord, the results are loss of bowel and bladder control and sexual function and impaired sensation below the level of damage. The injury may be complete or incomplete. The usual time frame to see if any movement will return is about one year. If no movement returns it is called "complete."

There is no cure for spinal cord injury. Nevertheless, the injured person requires good medical and nursing care, supportive measures to maximize movement and prevent infection plus lots of love. The family is a foundation, a secure ground upon which we stand together.

My husband and I were at Rick's bedside constantly. This was the beginning of a long and heartbreaking journey for us, but it was nothing compared to the painful and courageous journey on which Rick was about to embark.

Perhaps we would not have survived without the support we received from our families, friends, Rick's fellow lifeguards, clergy, medical personal and my husband's fellow fire-fighters. Even the housekeeping staff at the hospital made sure we were as comfortable as possible. There were several articles in the local newspaper about the accident, and most of my friends called my home to inquire about Rick's condition. With each call that came, I cried more. My mother called every day and I again cried. She was concerned about my mental health and tried to console me.

"Rick will be alright because he has his mind," she told me several times.

I was a basket case. When I met friends at the supermarket, I couldn't speak to them, I just cried. I carried on for a long time with this "crying jag." My wonderful mother sent meals to my home every day and my sisters helped me maintain my home. I received a lot of support from my family. I have a tremendous love for my children, and the sadness that this horrible accident caused made my love even greater.

After the first week of being hospitalized, Rick asked, with lip movements only, that a barber shave his entire head. He had a head of heavy, curly hair that needed to be shampooed daily. Lying on his back, unable to move, made this task difficult. This was one sign of his courage. The hair styles at this time were long.

"What kind of a haircut do you want?" the barber asked.

Rick silently mouthed the words, "Cut it all off."

Rick stayed in the Intensive Care Unit for three weeks. Their rules were two visitors at a time; therefore, our family took turns waiting outside and relieving one another.

After the initial shock wore off, I began to do some thinking. "How can this tragic situation be transformed into something positive?"

"I have an idea, I'll write a book," I said to myself.

As a first step, I decided to take a picture of Rick in traction. So I asked the nurse if I could take a picture of my son. But the nurse said that photographs were not allowed.

This did not stop me. I decided to make a log of his daily activities while in the hospital that I kept until he was discharged. Each day when I arrived home I sat at my typewriter and typed until I had a log over two inches thick. This helped me, in a way, to relieve some of my stress.

Rick's condition stabilized after three weeks. He was moved into a lovely private room close to the nurse's station in an orthopedic ward.

"Your doing so well, we're giving you a promotion," the doctor said.

He now could have as many visitors that he could tolerate. I received a call from a friend, Rita Croteau, whose son, Charles, had a spinal cord injury a year earlier after a trampoline accident. She gave me lots of encouragement.

"He will improve in time. It's not like he has a disease such as cancer when things usually get worse.

"Charles had rehab at Boston University Hospital where they were excellent. I would advise it for anyone," she said.

It was not long after, when Rick had a special visitor—Charles. He came wheeling into the room, and Rick seemed somewhat uneasy about his appearance. Charles was pleasant enough, but I could see my son was frightened. It was as if he was thinking, "Is this going to be my life too?"

Charles did not stay too long. I called Rita and thanked her. She was a fantastic lady and had won the "Teacher of the Year Award" in the city.

Rick received excellent care at Worcester City Hospital.

The nurses and doctors were compassionate and I could sense they felt as helpless as we did. They knew there was no cure for Rick's type of injury.

We spent most of each day with Rick arriving first thing in the morning to help give him nourishment. As we fed him he often had a remark to make such as, "It's a good thing my taste buds didn't get numb too, that would be awful."

Rick was sleeping poorly and that gave him time to do a lot of thinking. Each morning when we arrived he often complained.

"Last night was worse than the night before. I didn't sleep at all."

Ten days after his accident we had a wonderful surprise. Rick was able to raise his hand.

I read his lips as he mouthed, "Look, I can touch my nose but it's like lifting a hundred pound weight."

This new movement made it possible for nurses to set up a gadget so Rick could drink by himself. A pitcher of water was placed lower than his bed. Several feet of tubing ran from the pitcher to a glass connecting tube which was taped to the palm of his hand. Now Rick just had to move his arm muscles to get that hand to his mouth. He proudly showed us how he could do it. He had to work terribly hard for a sip of water. Both my husband and I struggled to hold back our tears.

To give him encouragement I said, "You will have a better night after working this hard."

The tracheotomy tube was removed after two weeks. He was no longer in danger of getting pneumonia. It left a hole in his neck.

"It will close in time," the doctors said.

It was a positive happening and now Rick could finally speak. He had another chest X-ray. When the technician asked him to "take a deep breathe and hold it," Rick's reply was, "How do you hold your breath when you have a hole in your throat?"

Since he was placed in a private room he received many visitors including the Brothers from St. John's High School, his girlfriend, Bonnie, many boy friends and all his relatives. When his friends first came to see him, and walked into his room, the expressions on their faces and the sadness in their eyes showed they were shocked to see Rick in this condition. His shaved head was held in Barton tongs which looked like ice tongs and were secured by small holes drilled in his skull. The weights, which hung from the tongs, provided traction for his vertebrae. His arms and legs were immobile and bottles dripped into his bladder in order to irrigate it. It was not a pleasant sight. But Rick's friends soon became accustomed to the situation and started to select favorite tapes for the player we had set up in his room. After the visit one of the boys shook Rick's hand to say good-bye but it was not a handshake. There was no movement there at all.

Each day his neurosurgeon checked his feeling level by sticking him with a needle only to find no improvement. My husband and I often left the hospital with heavy hearts, as we never heard a good report. But there was one positive note. His general condition was good. His appetite was excellent and he was usually in good spirits.

"Take it one day at the time. And keep the faith," I often said.

He was lucky his diaphragm was not affected, but he had paralyzed chest muscles and had to receive inhalation therapy every day. The complications from spinal cord injuries are numerous. He had frequent chest X-rays to check for pneumonia; he was given blood-thinning medication to prevent blood clots that sometimes occur with inactive extremities; and he was monitored for urinary tract infections. He also received a lumber puncture which showed bloody spinal fluid, a bad sign.

The doctors were doing everything possible to keep Rick free from complications. One troublesome problem was that he was feverish every day and the doctors did not know why. The high fevers often made him feel too sick to eat. Fortunately, he was always good about taking liquids, which was important to keep the fever somewhat in check. The weather did not help either because it was an extremely hot and humid summer, and there was no air conditioning in the hospital. It wasn't until the Barton tongs were removed after six weeks when the fever finally subsided.

Rick observed his eighteenth birthday on August twenty-first lying on his back motionless in his hospital bed. The nurses, his girlfriend, Bonnie, and his family sang "Happy Birthday" around his big birthday cake. There were flowers, cards, pizzas and soft drinks. Rick was happy.

Bonnie brought some special holy oil for use in time of sickness. I suggested a drop on each extremity.

"I'll have the nurse put it on my arms and legs in the morning after I have my bath," Rick said.

Rick told me he had been praying a lot since he was injured. "I've prayed to Him all my life and He has never let me down. I talk to God in my own words not the type of prayers you read out of a book. I know He hears me," he said.

I left him with a happy feeling in my heart, knowing his

thoughts were still positive and that he left it all in the capable hands of God.

A portable window fan and a television set were added to his room. When we left Rick for the night, we arranged things around the room for his comfort. We made sure the fan was set properly, all the lights out, the water gadget was tied to his hand, and there was plenty of ice water in the pitcher. There was no way he could call the nurse, so she tied a bell on his wrist. He could raise his arm enough to make the bell ring. My husband and I usually left Rick for the evening, with our heads down. We would cry on our way home. Then we would arrive at six the next morning to feed him breakfast.

Each day his extremities were exercised. The physiotherapist did a set and later I would do a set. Rick began to complain about soreness he felt in his shoulders. I explained that the soreness was from lack of use, and that it was similar to football stiffness that will disappear with exercise.

Slowly Rick began eating and sleeping better, although he still ran a fever. Bonnie, Jack, his girlfriend Gina, and Rick, friends who once doubled dated, now often gathered around his bed laughing and talking. This was his best therapy.

One day I noticed the color of his urine was red. The nurse already knew and a blood count was ordered for the morning. His blood pressure was checked and his bladder was irrigated. He had developed a urinary tract infection, which is common in this type of an injury. He was immediately given medication for the infection.

The doctors had planned to operate to do a spinal fusion so he could be taken out of traction but since his tracheotomy hole was still open, they decided to wait.

At one point Rick decided to stop taking sleeping pills because he believed they were causing him to have weird dreams. I suggested trying his old favorite, cookies and milk before bedtime.

I had a brief chat with our friend Dr. Bianchi, in the corridor. He said there were two other people being treated for accidents similar to Rick's, and that Rick was showing the most improvement. I had to tell Rick this.

The days were very hot, 90 degrees and humid. Rick especially suffered from the heat. His injury interfered with his perspiring. He only perspired above the injury and did not perspire below it. Gina and I applied cold compresses on his body as well as directed the fan on him to cool him off. There was often no relief from the heat throughout the night.

When I arrived one morning, Rick told me that he felt terrible. He had had a bad night, his head ached and his tongs and throat hurt. I reassured him that he had to expect a few bad days once in awhile. I told him he would be all right and that his condition would improve. I left him for a short time.

When I returned later in the afternoon, he was stripped naked except for a six by six inch square pad over his genitals. He was lying motionless on his back with the fan blowing on him. Ice bags had been placed under each arm and on each groin. There was a basin of half water half alcohol to bathe his entire body. Three doctors came in to see him. A throat culture was ordered. It showed he had strep throat and an ear infection. Large doses of antibiotics were administered and within a few hours his temperature was down. I told him to ask God to help him today.

"But Mom, I have already, three times so far this morning," he said.

Although my heart was heavy seeing Rick suffer so, I was glad to hear that he had such faith in God.

On another occasion, Rick was so sick that he asked that his girlfriend not visit him that day. My husband, Tony, spent the night with him. Tony put a couple of chairs together and tried to doze. He tied a bell on Rick's wrist to alert him in case he needed something. His usual request was for a drink of water. Rick was so sick this time that he was not able to raise his arms to his mouth with the water gadget. And Tony was there all night making sure Rick had enough fluids. I'm sure Rick appreciated this, because he is that type of person.

When I arrived the next morning, I found Rick feeling better but drowsy from a poor night's sleep. My husband looked as white as a sheet. I decided to see if all of Rick's treatments could be given about the same time so he could rest an hour or so in between. It was difficult but I got Rick to catnap a few times. I sat outside his closed door with a "No Visitors" sign posted clearly in view. I only let three people enter his room at one time, the medication nurse, the inhalation therapist and the nurse who gave him his daily bath. I stopped anyone who tried to enter while he was napping. Tony and I relieved each other so that Rick always had one of us with him.

The next day Rick was eating well, a sign he was feeling better. It took the nurse about two hours to give him morning care. It was not an easy task to handle my son with all his disabilities. He was unable to turn or raise himself in any way. The nurse who was caring for him had to do every move herself usually with the assistance of another nurse. Rick continued running a fever and I was concerned. I felt he was losing ground. The fever was making him sluggish and weak. It would take a long time to regain the small movement he had to take a sip of water. Brother Fahey, one of Rick's teachers, was amazed at Rick's courage and felt that Rick put us all to shame with our petty complaints. He marveled at Rick's disposition. He said that he never found Rick depressed or feeling sorry for himself and that we should be proud of him.

Finally Rick's fever had come down, so Tony and I felt we could both go home for the night.

One morning Rick told us a sad story. He had called for the nurse for one hour and no one heard him. He said he finally decided, "The heck with it, I'll go through the night thirsty and forget about it."

He prayed for someone to come but no one came.

These little stories made me realize over and over again how helpless he was. It was heartbreaking.

Rick was faced with another problem, a skin rash. He had pimples with pustules over his entire face. The skin specialist saw him and attributed it to cortisone that had been given to him on admission. An antiseptic type of medication was prescribed, but it did not help.

Rick's feet began to show reddened areas, a sure sign of pressure sores. It disturbed me to see this because bedsores are difficult to treat. At home, I felt terribly blue over these set backs. I cried at the supper table and could not eat. I was physically and mentally exhausted.

I did not go to see Rick that evening. I was too depressed. I stayed home, went to my room, prayed and cried.

My son, Bob, came home to find me in this depressed state and comforted me, "You can be sure everything that can be done is being done and we're all coping as well as can be expected," he said.

I cried until there were no more tears to shed. It was as if I had struck the bottom of a well. I had used up all the tears, and I was left with an amazing emptiness inside.

It was like having a bad case of the flu. I was exhausted, bone tired. There was an empty place in my rib cage and I wondered how an empty space could feel so heavy.

The next day I pulled myself together and went to the hospital as usual. When I left to go home for supper, I walked out to the parking lot. A police car was sitting there. It seemed strange, but I ignored it and went on looking for my car. I could not find it.

"Are you looking for your car?" a police officer asked.

"Yes. It was parked right here," I said, pointing to the parking space where an old junk car now sat in place of mine.

"Your car must have been stolen, lady. Maybe they dropped this one off in its place," he said.

My car was a sporty light green 1972 Mustang, the same car Rick had taken on his dates with Bonnie.

I called my husband and told him what happened and he picked me up. How important is a car? Having my car stolen was nothing compared to what my son was going through. I had learned to put things in their proper prospective. The car was found a few hours later totally stripped. It wasn't long before it was repaired and returned in good running order.

Rick had a fever for two weeks and the doctors were puzzled. His lungs were clear, and he didn't have a urinary infection. However, the doctor who examined Rick on this particular day found his abdomen was badly distended. His orders were for no food, an X-ray of the abdomen and intravenous feedings. The "no food" hardly pleased Rick. The following day, as the X-ray was negative, the intravenous was discontinued and his regular diet was resumed.

Rick's hair was beginning to grow and needed to be shampooed. His face and head were beginning to get very itchy. I had to wash his hair. It wasn't easy to wash a head that has to remain flat and had tongs on each side. A waterproof pad was put under his head and my daughter and I managed to shampoo his hair. I am sure he felt much better. His face was washed and special ointment applied but his face continued to itch. It was horrible that Rick was unable to scratch the itch. He tried intensely to dismiss it from his mind. The intense itch concerned both my husband and me. It seemed to us that a person with an itch who couldn't scratch it might become insane. Along with the rash, Rick continued to have a fever and he was still sleeping poorly.

There were other problems. Dr. Stone, the neurologist, who was to remove Rick's traction and perform a spinal fusion, had an emergency appendectomy operation and he was admitted to the sixth floor.

Rick was terribly disappointed that his own operation was postponed. When the noon meal arrived, Rick did not want to eat. His abdomen was still distended, so he only ate soup. This was the first time he had eaten so poorly. After I fed Rick his lunch I went home. The phone rang several times, but I still could not speak without crying.

Tony called me to come back to the hospital. Rick was itching so badly that he wanted his head washed again. I hurried back to the hospital and washed his hair with a special dandruff shampoo. This made him comfortable for a little while. We turned off the lights and settled Rick for the night. Tony and I went home exhausted.

The next morning, Rick was a lot worse. His face was red with pustules and pimples everywhere—not a pleasant sight to see on such a handsome face. Rick still itched and his temperature was still elevated. He was extremely uncomfortable. I applied cold compresses to his face to relieve the itch, but it didn't help. The weather continued to be too hot and humid which didn't help either. We did everything possible to try to help keep him cool. He did not wear a hospital Johnnie but lay in bed naked with a sheet covering his genitals and a fan blowing on him as before.

It was seven weeks since his accident and the first time I saw sadness in Rick's beautiful brown eyes. He was having a bad week. His doctor was operated on for an appendectomy, Bonnie was occupied by nurse's training at a local hospital, and his rash got worse. He had hoped that this week would be the week when he would be taken out of traction and would start to sit up.

Since the tragic dive, depression had become second nature to me. I was no longer remembered as a happy person, I couldn't remember the last time I had laughed. I would often break down sobbing. My older son comforted me. He patted my back and tried to reassure me.

"Rick is one of God's children. He'll take care of him," Bob said.

Rick's progress remained the same. Each day the doctors would check his feeling level. They would start at his toes, touching him with a sharp instrument and working their way up his entire body until they reached his mid chest area.

Each time Rick was asked, "Do you feel this?"

And each time he answered, "No."

Rick's feeling started at mid-chest level. All other parts of his body had no feeling. Doctor Stone had not seen him for a week and Rick was anxious to be taken out of traction. He had more bad days than good days because of discomfort in his shoulder. X-rays of the shoulders were ordered and they showed bursitis. Hot packs were used to relieve the discomfort. The rash on his face looked worse. It was disfiguring with redness and pustule pimples everywhere. He was tortured by the intense itching the rash had produced.

A week later Dr. Stone was finally discharged as a patient. The doctor was in his early fifties, about six feet tall, medium build with a good crop of brown hair beneath which was a brilliant mind. I often heard nurses say, "If I were unconscious after an accident, I would want Dr. Stone to be my doctor."

The nurses and patients liked him. He was kind, compassionate, friendly and knowledgeable in his field. Our family had complete confidence in his decisions. It was mid-morning when the doctor walked slowly into Rick's room. He was favoring his left side and he held a huge bouquet of assorted cut flowers. He placed the flowers on the bedside table.

"These are for you, Rick," he said with a smile.

"Thank you. I've missed you Doc," Rick responded, smiling.

They were both so happy to see one another. The doctor immediately ordered the traction removed and a neck brace to replace it. He also ordered elastic stocking to be worn at all times to prevent blood clots. It was a relief for Rick to have that traction removed. It was the initial step toward sitting up and getting out of bed.

Before long a technician from a prosthetic company came to measure Rick for a brace. A few hours later he arrived with the brace. It came in two pieces, a back and a front with two straps over each shoulder, and an eight-inch bar across the front of the chest. It had two hooks, one on each side of the neck part to facilitate its removal or to secure it in place. There was a section that fit beneath his chin. The technician explained it to Rick and stressed the importance of keeping it clean and dry so it would not irritate his skin. Rick had been lying flat on his back for over six weeks looking at the white ceiling and watching some television. It was a happy time. He was finally going to be able to have his bed elevated into a sitting position.

After spending all this time in one position, I must give accolades to the nurses who worked very hard to keep the skin on his back healthy. He had no bedsores, which are common in this type of a case. In my nursing career I have seen sores that were so deep and severe that skin grafts had to be performed.

With the traction removed, we thought Rick would be more comfortable—but that was not the case. The brace was extremely uncomfortable. It dug into Rick's chest and into his skin. The only one who could adjust it was the technician and he was not always available.

It was Labor Day weekend and a skeletal staff was working in the entire hospital. Rick was in agony with the brace digging into him. I was desperate to find someone who could help my son. I roamed around the hospital until I found a personal friend, Dr. Albert Haddad, an orthopedic surgeon making his rounds. The doctor was a tall, handsome, dark haired fellow in his mid-fifties. The nurses thought he looked like Cary Grant. I met him near the emergency room and asked him to come to my son's room on the third floor.

"Doctor, could you please help my son, his brace is killing him," I said.

"I'll be glad to do anything I can," he said.

When he arrived and assessed the situation, he could easily see the problem.

He went to the kitchen and got a table knife that he could use like a screwdriver.

He made a little adjustment that made a big difference. Rick immediately felt better. His chin was where it was supposed to be and nothing was binding. Although the brace was more comfortable, Rick remained miserably sick with a fever, itchy rash and painful shoulders. The dermatologist ordered a sulfur ointment but soon found it was not working. Several ointments were tried but were equally unsuccessful. The rash remained ugly and itchy.

In the evenings Rick often had a room full of visitors. His friends and girlfriend came regularly but he never complained to them. He smiled, gabbed and joked pretending he was feeling well. They played tapes and gave him news of the day. He enjoyed that very much. He had a loyal gang of boys who stuck by him through this tragic time. They kept him company until the nurses came into his room to settle him for the night.

Now that Rick was out of traction, it was time for him to advance to a tilt table in the physiotherapy department. This was to prepare his body to tolerate getting out of bed. He looked forward to this new experience. It was a step forward, a more positive approach to his recovery. A kind orderly came with a stretcher to take him to the physiotherapy department. Rick was dressed for the first time. He wore a Johnnie and green hospital pants. The three-way catheter and bottle of irrigating solution went with him while he was lifted onto the stretcher. A slot on the stretcher accommodated the drainage system of the catheter.

A tilt table is a specially designed table, which allows the patient to gradually become accustomed to an upright position. Transferring Rick to a stretcher was not an easy task. A lifting sheet was placed under him to ease the transfer to the stretcher and later to the tilt table. With Rick's muscles in a relaxed state and his entire body like a limp rag, it took four people to transfer him.

There was one person at his head, one on each side of the lifting sheet and one at his feet. The entire process was far more efficient with five people because the fifth person carried the urine bag and irrigating bottle.

Once Rick was transferred to the table, he was strapped down with one large strap over his chest and another one over his knees; a flat pillow was placed under his head for comfort and a thick pad place under his feet. With a flip of a switch, the table began to rise into an upright position. Slowly with intermittent stops the table was raised about ten degrees. After about five minutes he asked to be lowered. It was dropped down five degrees. Fifteen minutes later he asked to be lowered again. He was beginning to feel dizzy and sick to his stomach. The table was lowered to the flat level and after a rest period it was raised to thirty-five degrees. The technician praised Rick for his first day; he had accomplished a significant height.

So ended the two-hour visit to the physiotherapy department. Rick was wheeled to his room in time for lunch, but he could not eat. His stomach was upset.

Rick was placed on the tilt table every day. He could remain at thirty degrees for seven minutes, forty degrees for nine minutes and forty-five degrees for three minutes. He would have to reach ninety degrees to be able to sit up in a chair.

The time had come to start making arrangements for Rick's transfer to the rehab hospital. We decided on Boston University Hospital, which has an excellent spinal cord injury unit. The hospital is about forty miles from our home and convenient for family and friends to visit. We felt it was a good choice.

Tony and I drove to Boston to tour the spinal cord unit and meet with Dr. Murray Freed, the head of the department. The spinal cord unit was located in the Robinson Building. The building and the wards were old and dreary looking. Beds were lined up with only a curtain between them for privacy. However, I knew that the care and compassion there were unsurpassed. The personnel were outstanding. The staff was like a close knit family.

While we waited to consult with Dr. Freed, we spoke to Kelley the head of the occupational department. She was happy to hear that I was a registered nurse and had some knowledge of spinal cord injuries. The doctor's secretary led us into Dr. Freed's Office. It was small and not elaborately furnished with a simple desk and some files. Dr. Freed was a very personable man. He was in his fifties and neatly dressed in a dark suit. As he greeted us, I noticed he was wearing a prosthesis on one leg. Apparently he was a casualty of World War II. He showed a great deal of compassion toward us and he listened carefully as we explained our son's condition. He had already spoken to Dr. Stone.

Our conference was brief. Dr. Freed told us that Rick could be admitted to the unit as soon as Monday when a bed became available. He said that he would make all the arrangements for the transfer. We left his office and slowly went to our car for our return trip home. Neither of us spoke on the drive back to Worcester. We were sad and frightened.

What were we going to do...?

What could we do?

The trip to Boston took a good part of the day but we arrived at the hospital at four o'clock in time to feed Rick his supper. The ward was filled to capacity and the nurses were very busy, so I became Rick's nurse temporarily. I changed his position by placing him on his side with a pillow propped against his back, gave him a back rub, set his television so he could view it, told him about his transfer to the University Hospital on Monday and settled him for the night by turning off his lights and leaving him fresh water. Both Tony and I arrived home physically and mentally drained.

Summer vacation was over and the children were back to school. Bob left to start his third year at the University of Bridgeport in Connecticut, which meant that I lost my dearest supporter. I missed him more then ever. Whenever he saw me crying he put his arm around my shoulders and said kind words to console me.

"Don't cry, Mom, we are a family and we have a lot to offer Rick. We can work together to help him."

Bob had as much sadness in his heart as I had and yet he had this wonderful attitude. My husband and I were fair with our children treating them as unique individuals. At first as a result of Rick's injury, we were not able to attend all the children's school functions. As Rick's health improved; we became active again. I think it helped a great deal. Bob and Gina have no resentment toward the attention we have given their brother. They support him with frequent visits and make sure that he has everything he needs.

Rick was pleasantly surprised when Bob would make a special trip home from college to visit him. And Bob, as usual, was ready to comfort us with his consoling words.

One morning, after the nurse finished Rick's morning care, she decided he needed a change of scenery. She wheeled his bed out of his room and into a large sunny solarium overlooking a busy parking lot. His bed was elevated into a sitting position, so he could view the activity in front of the hospital. In spite of all this, Rick was very sad. He was not smiling as he usually was. Apparently he had requested to see himself in a mirror. The face in the mirror was not his face but a red, pus infested, pimply mass of skin. His disfigured face disturbed him a great deal.

The nurses had been wonderful to Rick. They catered to all his needs with a smile. They were always pleasant and willing to help in any way possible to make my son comfortable. Our family could not have asked for a more compassionate group of nurses.

Rick had been in the hospital for nine weeks when he was due to leave for Boston. On his last night in the general hospital he had a room full of friends. Bonnie arrived and took first place at his bedside. They all had a great time chatting and playing his favorite songs. The place was full of merriment. It set the stage for a good night's rest before his busy day on the morrow.

CHAPTER FOUR

A SNAPSHOT OF TONY

In 1945, Tony had recently been discharged from the Air Corps where he had served as a fighter pilot. He was visiting his 96-year-old maternal grandmother who was in Worcester City Hospital with pneumonia. I was a student nurse working the 3 to 11 P.M. shift in an open geriatric ward. We were instructed to inform visitors that visiting hours ended at 9 P.M. When I made the announcement, Tony came to me and said that he could stay longer because his grandmother was on the danger list.

Tony kept coming to see his grandmother. If I wasn't on duty he would inquire about my whereabouts. When I saw him again, our conversation went beyond his grandmother's condition. I thought he was handsome. He had a warm personality, a pleasing smile, and he was very charming. He asked me for a date, and I accepted. We began by going out for a cold drink a few times, but later we went out for an evening which included fine dining. But the evenings ended at ten when I had to be back in the nurses' quarters for curfew.

When I received flowers on Valentine's Day, I felt that I was special to him.

Tony attended my graduation ceremony and presented me with a dozen American Beauty Roses. We got engaged shortly thereafter, but we waited a year to get married because I wanted to earn some money, which I did by working as a private duty nurse.

He was twenty-seven years old and I was twenty-two when we were married. We have been married for over five decades.

At the time of Rick's tragic accident Tony was in his early fifties. He was stocky and athletically built but not a big man. He was average height and weight with dark skin and hair. His fine features were like the popular Italian singers Perry Como and Dean Martin—a handsome dude. In his high school years, he was an outstanding halfback for the Commerce High School football team. He was popular throughout the city for his excellent performance in football.

When the children were in their early teens we joined the Holden Country Club as a family. Here Tony played his finest golf. He played to a one handicap, winning the club championship and was invited to several pro-amateur tournaments. This was a fun time for all of us, just months before the tragic accident. Thank the Lord we had no inkling of the terrible tragedy in our future.

He was the finest dad any child could have. When our children were infants, he changed their diapers and fed them as expertly as any mother. He gave them his undivided attention. We went on several family vacations, to the New York World's Fair, Niagara Falls, and Florida.

Tony never gave the children long lectures. He was a man of few words, but those he said were powerful such as "If I catch you drinking and driving I will take the keys and your license." The children adored him.

When the tragedy happened, Tony's world tipped over on its side with no way of righting it. He covered up his emotions by keeping himself busy making things to improve Rick's quality of life. The accident broke Tony's heart but he tried hard to be brave.

CHAPTER FIVE

OFF TO REHABILITATION

It was a perfect day. The sky was blue without a cloud, and the temperature was mild—a welcome change from the unbearably hot and humid weather of August. It was September eighteenth, nine weeks after Rick's accident, and Rick was to be transferred to the spinal cord unit at Boston University Hospital, a division of Boston University Medical School. It was a day of hope for my son.

His departure from City Hospital was an emotional one. Dozens of medical personnel came into his room to see him off and wish him well. The devoted, compassionate nurses bid him good-bye. Some kissed him on the cheek—which went over big with my son. Among the staff, there were mixed emotions. They were glad to see him leave to get the intensive therapy he needed to help him attain a reasonable life style. But many of the medical people said they would miss Rick. He had been a good patient usually joking and smiling and always appreciative of anything that was done for him. And the nurses tried to brighten his days by telling him little jokes.

Mary Levine, the efficient and likable head nurse on JM 3, was there seeing to it that the transfer was accomplished properly. Mary ran a tight ship and the patients benefited from it. Rick was a perfect example. He was free of bedsores despite the fact he had been lying in bed for nine weeks.

On the morning of his transfer, Rick was given a mild tranquilizer to help with the stress of the change. Mary handed me a large manila envelope containing his X-rays and another smaller envelope with a photostatic copy of his hospital chart and a nurse's summary which I was to give to Dr. Freed at the University Hospital.

The decision to transfer Rick had not been done without a lot of research. I wanted to make very sure that the ambulance company had a good safety record and that the ambulance was clean and well staffed.

When the two attendants arrived they did their work under the watchful eyes of our family. Tony, Gina, and I got into the elevator with the two men and Rick on the stretcher. We marched down several long corridors to the emergency room door where the ambulance was waiting. Rick was carefully lifted into the ambulance with his head toward the front while I was given a seat next to him. I rode in the ambulance with Rick while Gina and my husband followed in our car. Bob was away at college.

Neither Rick nor I said much on the trip. Rick was mildly sedated and I was doing more thinking than talking. I looked out the window and saw the trees and passing cars, knowing all too well that Rick could not move his head or see anything but the roof of the ambulance. I was keenly aware of every bump on the highway because each one caused Rick a good deal of pain.

The amount of sensitivity in his upper body seemed to have increased. This was probably due to the lack of sensitivity in his lower body—much like how a blind person can hear and feel much more than a person with sight.

He wore a brace that dug into his skin, even though it had been adjusted to make it more comfortable, and the rash on his face continued to cause extreme itching. It was only a forty-five mile trip in light traffic, but it seemed much longer. Sometimes when we hit a bump, Rick would just close his eyes. Sometimes I would too. There was nothing else I could do.

When we finally reached Boston, Rick was lifted out of the ambulance and moved to his room. Tony and I went into the doctor's office and I handed my son's records to Dr. Freed.

Dr. Freed and another doctor looked at the X-rays. "It's a shame that there's no fracture here. It's just a dislocation of the fifth and sixth vertebrae and unfortunately substantial damage to the spinal cord," Dr. Freed said to the other doctor.

Dr. Freed also took note of Rick's weakened condition at the time of the accident. About a month before the accident, Rick had had knee surgery and developed a low grade fever, his appetite was poor and he had lost fifteen pounds.

At the time of his transfer, Rick had spent seven weeks in Barton tongs with twenty-eight pounds of traction and two weeks in a cervical brace. Approximately six weeks out of the nine he had had a low grade fever. He also developed an ear and throat infection, as well as an infection where one of the tongs was inserted into his skull. He was experiencing severe itching from the rash on his back, chest and face, and his shoulders ached.

Rick was admitted to a twelve-bed ward. A cloth curtain separated each bed and allowed limited privacy. One could hear what was said and the activities on the other side of the curtain. The other patients were aware that a new patient was being admitted and they were naturally curious. We arrived in time for lunch. The menu was veal parmigiana. The other patients teased Rick saying that the hospital personnel knew a handsome, young Italian boy was coming so they prepared Italian food in his honor.

In the bed next to Rick was a sixteen-year-old boy, Chris, who also had broken his neck in a diving accident. It seemed a frightening coincidence. It was too soon for conversation between them. Neither spoke. As time went on these two became great buddies, exchanged small talk and discussed their conditions. The two boys seemed to be of special interest to the interns. They were often taken to a conference room and placed side by side on their beds while the doctors discussed their injuries. Chris was the same level as Rick but he could do more, for instance, he was able to turn the knob on his television set, which Rick was not able to do. It proved how different the affects of this injury could be. Rick listened closely to all the doctors' comments and learned a great deal about his condition.

✿   ✿   ✿

That first day was traumatic for us all—new surroundings, new medical personnel, a new routine, and finding our way around the hospital. It was all new, and without realizing it, we were anxious.

The first thing that happened was a positive sign. A nurse immediately removed Rick's uncomfortable neck brace and replaced it with a large towel folded in fours. This gave Rick much needed relief.

While the nurse fed Rick his dinner, we went to the hospital cafeteria for our lunch. We said very little. Several times Gina's eyes filled with tears. It was terribly sad to see so many young people without the use of their arms and legs.

It was at this moment that my son truly realized the severity of his injury. His future in a wheelchair must have looked dreadfully grim. When we arrived back at his bedside, Rick was silent. He stared at the ceiling in deep thought. It was the first day in the new setting. We all suffered.

We spent as much time with Rick as we could. The nurses turned him every two hours to relieve pressure on his back and prevent bedsores. Back rubs were not given here as in the general hospital. They relied on the turning procedure.

While waiting outside the room, I met Chris's mother, a minister's wife from Laconia, New Hampshire. She was lovely, well groomed, in her mid-forties with lots of wisdom. We sat and chatted.

"All we can do for our boys is to pray," she said.

It was comforting to talk to her. The first day was the toughest, she said, and she added that it would soon get better.

✤   ✤   ✤

Many things fascinated Rick. For example, he was intrigued by the electric thermometer that was used, and this sort of interest helped buoy his spirits. We stayed to feed him supper. He ate well including two servings of milk, but then a voice from behind one of the curtains said that too much milk could cause calcium deposits in the kidneys. So Rick switched to tea.

The next morning, Rick was already booked to have an intravenous pyelogram—an X-ray of the kidneys. Dye is put into the veins to give them an outline. And Rick was to have two enemas, one that evening and one in the morning.

The first day was finally coming to an end. We arranged the television set on his nightstand so he could view it easily. We kissed him goodnight and left for home with heavy hearts.

CHAPTER SIX

PROGRESS

With Rick's move to Boston, we had a new schedule to get used to. Visiting hours at the center were from 1 to 8 P.M. In the mornings, the patients received intensive therapy in an effort to restore some movement to their paralyzed bodies. When we arrived in Boston on Rick's second day, he told us just how hectic his morning had been. He had gone to X-ray for the intravenous pyelogram. The doctor arrived very late, so Rick had time to chat with the technician. In his typical fashion, Rick asked her question after question. The technician told him all about the X-ray machine and its operation. She also told him that she was amazed at how quickly he understood what she had taken years to learn.

The doctor was blunt. He said that in most cases, people with injuries like Rick's spend the rest of their lives in wheelchairs. But we held on to the word "most" and never gave up hope.

Another doctor who examined Rick was impressed with Rick's attitude. He assured us that a positive attitude would do more good than all the therapy combined. The doctor said that often a patient's mental condition was so awful that psychiatric treatment was necessary.

We knew our son was determined to walk again. The nurses too were delighted with his marvelous attitude and personality. They called him "Angel of the Dorm."

On the second afternoon there was little conversation. We were all contemplating what the future had in store for us. What would the future hold for Rick? Would he ever recover? And if he did not, what sort of life would he have, and what sort of life would we have? Could we handle whatever was coming down the road?

Later in the evening things got livelier. Most of the patients had visitors. I suggested that Rick telephone Bonnie. We placed a pillow under the earpiece of the phone so he could speak to her. As he chatted he had a smile from ear to ear.

Rick's technical mind immediately came up with ideas to make life a little easier for everyone. For instance, he suggested that two earpieces be attached to his television set so he would hear only his television. This was easily done and pleased him, and Rick was in good spirits when we left for home around nine o'clock.

The next day I stayed home while Tony drove into Boston. (Each day either Tony or I or both of us arrived in Boston in time to feed Rick his meals.) On his return, Tony told me Rick had had a good supper, was very talkative and seemed in good spirits. Rick seemed to enjoy the change.

This hospital was different from a general hospital. All efforts were slanted toward positive thinking. The staff put in a lot of time and energy to get their patients moving as much as possible. Many of the staff members had been there for years and were extremely knowledgeable about spinal cord injuries. It takes a special type of person to give these patients care. They moved slowly and spoke softly as if trying to create a calm atmosphere. I made sure I listened carefully to whatever they told me about Rick and about his therapy.

The next day Rick was scheduled to have his spine and lungs X-rayed. I arrived in time to feed Rick his dinner. I brought along his high school yearbook, which he had not yet seen. While he was waiting his turn in the X-ray department, I showed him the book. It provided much needed entertainment.

After the X-rays were completed, Rick was placed on a stretcher and wheeled into the recreation room. It was a very large room. There were several low platforms covered with padded mats on which the patients were exercised by the therapist. Here Rick was fitted for wrist braces. The braces were made of light plastic that was softened in hot water so that the braces could be molded to his wrists. Once they were put on they kept his wrists from hanging limply.

Rick was silent while we were in the recreation room. On a table near us there were drills, screws and soft foam rubber for padding—a strange collection for a recreation room. Perhaps they reminded Rick of just how much his life had changed.

Back in his room, his dad, Gina and Bonnie came to visit him. Rick had not been talkative all day but this visit seemed to draw him out. He chatted and smiled like his old self.

On his fifth day, I found Rick sitting up in the rec room. It was the first time in nine weeks that he had sat up. Getting him into a sitting position took time and expertise. Each leg was wrapped in ace bandages. One leg was elevated, the other hung down. A many-tailed binder was wrapped around his abdomen. These procedures helped him to tolerate the change in position. He had been sitting up for several hours and he said that he felt fine. The back of the wheelchair was placed on two pillows and tipped back against a stand to relieve pressure on his bottom. I had never seen this done before, and I thought it was a great idea. The hospital had very creative solutions to all kinds of problems.

Two very strong and capable male attendants wheeled Rick back to the dorm and placed him into his bed. This was only his second day out of bed and he had been able to sit up for over seven hours. His former dizziness and upset stomach had disappeared. These problems appeared to be solved.

There was another triumph. Rick could now feed himself with a bent fork that was inserted in a splint attached to the palm of his hand. He also had access to a telephone. He was able to phone family and friends by using a splint attached to the phone to hold it in his hand similar to the way he held his fork. By using a pencil in his mouth he could dial the numbers.

One of Rick favorite uncles, an artist, made several artistic signs for him to hang around his bed in the small cubicle:

"Smile God loves you."

"I take one day at a time."

"Today is the first day of the rest of my life."

"Think positively."

"Smile and the world smiles with you, cry and you cry alone."

When the doctors read the signs they applauded.

Whenever I spoke to Dr. Freed, he praised my son's courage and attitude. I explained that Rick kept his suffering to himself. I thought that perhaps he blamed himself for the injury, and that is why he did not complain. Dr. Freed discounted that line of reasoning. He said many other patients did not respond like our son.

I asked the doctor if my son would walk again. He told me not to count on it and he urged me not to allow my son to hope that he would walk again.

Dr. Freed checked Rick over using the same procedure as in the general hospital. He used a sharp instrument to touch different areas of Rick's body to see if he had any feelings.

Sadly, Rick's answer was always, "No."

Another day Rick was sitting in his wheelchair in the rec room when I arrived. I kidded him about being my handsome son and he grinned. The therapist asked me to wait outside while she worked on him. They were helping him to become mobile by teaching him to ride in the wheelchair through corridors in the hospital and to learn how to handle the wheelchair alone on carpeted as well as smooth floors. It was his first attempt at this tough new task. He was instructed to push hard with his hands on the outer spokes of the chair's large wheels. I knew he was having a hard time because of the pain in his shoulders. He tried to push himself but most of the time the therapist had to help him along. She wanted Rick to push five times, stop to rest and then repeat. Each time she praised him for his efforts but Rick was very weak. He was able to push only one out of the five times. As I watched, I had great difficulty holding back my tears. It is terribly painful to watch a once healthy, strong, athletic son struggle to move a wheelchair just one foot forward.

At bedtime a different method was used to put Rick into bed. Instead of two people grabbing his arms and legs, which hurt Rick's shoulders, three people used a slide board to slide him onto the bed. This was a big improvement.

The next day I picked up Bonnie at the nurse's quarters to take her with me to Boston. When we arrived we found Rick sitting in the rec room. I let Bonnie walk in alone to surprise him. I could see a big smile on her face as she approached him and his smile was even bigger. They were left alone for a while. When suppertime came, Rick wanted to show off by feeding himself. A bent fork was attached to his left thumb because he is left-handed. The food was served in a special plate with high ridges around to keep it from falling off the plate as he tried to stab it. He was able to pierce the solid food and put it into his mouth. He was unable to manage the softer food, which had to be fed to him. Halfway through the meal he tired and was unable to finish his meal by himself. Bonnie fed him the rest.

The nurse was not happy when she saw Bonnie feeding Rick. Rick had been able to feed himself during the day. The nurse felt he should try harder. I defended Rick by saying that he had started out beautifully like a house afire but all of a sudden he tired. According to the nurse, he forgot to rest in between fork fills. What patience this all must take.

Now and then, a migraine headache would cause me to stay home while my husband visited Rick. When that happened I would telephone Rick. He usually sounded upbeat, but things were progressing slowly.

On weekends the therapy department was closed, so we would wheel him out of the hospital and around the block to give him a change of scenery.

Tony had difficulty the first time he tried to navigate the wheelchair down one curb and up another. One particular incident was frightening. As Tony was lowering the wheel-chair down a curb, the footrest got stuck. Rick started to slowly slide off the chair. With the lack of muscles in his torso, he was unable to brace himself the way a normal person would. My husband frantically called two passers-by and they helped get Rick back on the seat. Tony realized he could not navigate curbs unless Rick was tied to the chair. There could have been tragic consequences if strangers had not come to his aid.

One day when we all arrived in Boston, Rick was nowhere on the ward. We looked everywhere. Finally a nurse told us he was on the roof—a large flat area where many of the patients were sent to get some fresh air and view the Boston skyline. It was a nice, sunny, clear day and a number of patients were up on the roof. Rick was brought down, dressed in Sunday slacks. His hair was brushed and his rash had been treated. When he greeted us, he came toward us using both arms in a boxing motion to show us how he was improving. We clapped enthusiastically.

Tony, Bonnie, Gina and I took a stroll outdoors with Rick. This time he was tied to his wheelchair. Tony did the pushing but as usual found it tough to navigate the curbs. We toured a pretty flower garden and circled back toward the hospital. On our way, we heard someone call Bonnie's name. Behind us were two of Rick's friends from home. We met at an ideal time. We had a few more helping hands to get Rick back to the hospital. The boys and Bonnie spent most of the afternoon with Rick in the rec room while my husband and I watched a football game on television.

When the boys left for home, we used a technique with pillows to relieve the pressure on the base of Rick's spine. The pillows were put on a platform behind the wheelchair and the wheelchair was tipped backwards. Rick stayed in that position for an hour. To pass the time Gina, Bonnie, and Rick decided to work on a puzzle. Rick helped place several pieces by telling them where to put them.

After sitting up for several hours, Rick said he was tired and wanted to go to bed. He was wheeled to the bedside. I took off his shoes and socks and we put him to bed using the slide board. An orderly emptied his urine leg bag. While he was flat, all his clothes were removed. His tee shirt was slipped off one arm, then over his head and then off the other arm. His pants were slid off and the catheter was disconnected from his leg and reconnected to the bedside drainage bottle, which looked like an ordinary plastic gallon jug. He no longer needed the towel collar for support when he was lying down.

It was the first of October, two weeks since he arrived at the rehab hospital. We were pleased with his progress, but we still hoped for some more muscle movement. His coordination had improved as he got used to feeding himself. Nothing moved except his shoulder muscles. I was surprised how well he managed. If I tried to help him center the food on his plate, he became angry with me. He wanted to do it himself. But I felt frustrated when he struggled and had an overwhelming temptation to help him.

Rick had adjusted very well to his new surroundings, and it pleased us to see him smiling most of the time. We turned to prayer asking for a miracle. Our family recited the rosary each day and had attended daily mass every day since his accident. We prayed and prayed hoping for a miracle. We never gave up hope.

As part of his workout in the rec room, the physiotherapist instructed him to support himself while in a sitting position. While holding both his arms toward his back for support, he was pushed to see if he would fall over. He had enough strength in his shoulders to remain sitting. Rick was proud of this accomplishment.

Rick was always full with ideas. He requested some pread-dressed envelopes so he could type letters to Bonnie. He used an electric typewriter in this way. A large clip made out of white plastic material was attached to each hand. The clip had a hole in it to fit a pencil. The eraser side of the pencil was used to hit the keys. It took him a long time to type a few words but this was another sign of progress. The doctors were pleased and so were we.

Rick was given permission to leave the hospital for an over night stay at home on the weekend. It would be a great change for Rick but very tiring for Tony and me. The first thing the physiotherapist demonstrated was how to transfer him from his wheelchair to the car. The wheelchair arm was removed and the wheelchair placed close to the seat of the car. With our knees slightly flexed we grabbed Rick's trousers in the rear, made a pivot motion and dropped him onto the seat. Rick helped some by putting his arms around our neck. I was 110 pounds, Rick was approximately 140 pounds and I could do this maneuver without any trouble. It is a matter of body mechanics.

The third week of October marked Rick's first visit home since his accident. The first challenge was to lift Rick and the wheelchair up three steps to enter the house. The small vestibule was not large enough to turn the wheelchair—an area of at least five feet was needed—so Tony had to lift the wheelchair to a right angle to get into the house proper. Rick was grim-faced as he looked around. He was pleased to be home but being carried though the door brought back memories of when he was able to open the door and walk in. At this time renovations to the house had not been completed and so moving around with Rick was sometimes awkward and cumbersome.

The day was busy; he wanted to make some telephone calls to his girlfriend and friends. I made his favorite meal, Italian spaghetti with meatballs and sausage. He watched television and soon it was bedtime.

Tony lifted him out of the wheelchair into his bed, which was located next to the bedroom door. Tony and I took turns getting up at night to turn him every hour.

The next morning I was alone with Rick. Tony was at work, Bob was away at college and Gina was at her part-time job, but I felt confident, with my many years of nursing, to handle him without a problem—only this time he was not my patient but my eighteen-year-old son. I had to give him a bed bath washing his genitalia; inserting a rectal suppository to assist in his evacuation; irrigating the Foley catheter; disconnecting the bedside urine drainage system and connecting the catheter to the urinary bag that was attached to his leg; and dressing him like he was my baby. This embarrassed Rick terribly; he turned his head and never looked my way. I lifted him out of bed into his wheelchair to start his first full day at home. The weekend went by quickly and soon it was Sunday at three o'clock and we packed our supplies and headed back to Boston in time for him to receive his evening meal and settle him for the night.

❦   ❦   ❦

One day Rick was very talkative and very excited about some new items which had been ordered for him. First he was getting a new wheelchair. It was a standard size electric wheelchair. He had been using the hospital wheelchair. Now he would have one to call his own. Special features on the wheelchair would make things easier for him. There was a special footrest, a place on back of the chair to carry items such as his splints. It also had pneumatic tires, lower armrests, and could fit under a table. And to top it all off, there was a special gel pillow to sit on.

A special air mattress was also ordered, so that at night he only had to be turned every three hours instead of every two hours.

There was another innovation. Rick was weighed on a special scale so that he remained in his wheelchair. He weighed 140 pounds and did not want to gain weight. Any extra weight would make it more difficult for everyone when it came to lifting him.

Rick also liked chatting about what was going on with other patients. He told us about one of the patients who wanted to commit suicide. The patient told the physiotherapist that he was planning to slash his wrists. She went along with him in order to humor him but suggested that pills would be less messy. Rick got the biggest kick out of that story. He assured us that he was not going to give up, and he told us a more positive story about a man who had broken his back in two places and was now walking again with the help of a cane.

✤   ✤   ✤

Bob came home from college to visit his brother for the first time since Rick moved to Boston. When he got to the hospital he found that Rick was sick. During the night his catheter became plugged with a blood clot and backed up causing him to vomit and become very ill. Seeing him in this condition disturbed me badly, I cried all the way home. Bob consoled me, as usual.

"Mom, the most important thing is that Rick has a fine mind and can take this."

On top of everything, Rick's trip home for the weekend was cancelled because of his setback.

I knew that Bob was right. Rick could take it, but it seemed that he had an awful lot to take.

CHAPTER SEVEN

WAITING

The next time I visited Rick, I brought him a porterhouse steak smothered with onions. I felt it was about time for him to have some food from home. It was perfect timing because the menu that day was chipped beef over noodles—hardly one of Rick's favorites.

One weekend only four patients remained in the hospital while the other six went home for weekend visits. This was tough for those left behind. Every time we left for home, Rick was wheeled to the back door to see us off. He watched us wave good-bye, but he could not wave back. Someone with him had to do the waving for him.

One evening the patients suggested they all chip in to send out for pizzas since the day had been upsetting. The rec room had been unusable as the floors being washed and waxed. No therapy could take place. The patients were bored and missed that activity. The pizzas were a good idea to brighten the atmosphere.

After supper we played a game with Rick. It was 3-D tic

tack toe; a very interesting game. Rick won every time. He wasn't able to place the little tiles in the squares but told us exactly where he wanted them placed. The rec room was unusable for the second day, but the therapists kept their patients busy by practicing mobility. It was still terribly difficult for my son. I noticed he had bruised fingers from catching them in the rungs of the chair.

A staff conference was planned to discuss Rick's condition and possible discharge. We met with three of Rick's doctors, the occupational therapist, the physiotherapist and his nurse. There was dead silence when my husband and I entered the conference room hardly an encouraging sign. Dr. Freed, the chief of staff, was the first person to speak. He explained about the injury and the muscles Rick was able to use now. There were not many. His final dark words were that our son had damaged his spinal cord completely. However, there was a tiny ray of hope with slight movement now becoming evident in one wrist. Each one around the table took turns discussing Rick. The nurse and the therapists warned us that he would need total nursing care. He could do very little for himself. He could not bathe, dress himself, transfer out of the chair or turn the page of a book. At the present time, the only thing he could do was feed himself with the aid of a splint.

It was a very discouraging conference. They had nothing good to report. Nothing. I had braced myself the night before for such sad news, but the anticipation did not prevent my immense feeling of disappointment and even a little despair.

Rick had been complaining about soreness in his thumbs. I inquired hopefully about the possibility of this being a sign of returning feeling. The answer was negative and my small hope of normalcy returning to the thumbs quickly vanished. When Rick asked to hear the prognosis, we had to tell him the truth. All in all they really did not tell us anything we did not already know. On our way home neither Tony nor I spoke. We were in deep thought, in sadness and in prayer.

Rick and the therapists visited our home once to evaluate the structure and suggest changes to accommodate a wheel-chair. There were many things to consider. Both the occupa-tional therapist and the physiotherapist came with a check-list. It was a short visit just to look, measure and suggest.

As we carried out the inspection, we found the kitchen, living room and carpeted floor would not create a problem. But there were some problem areas. The bedroom and bath-room doors had to be widened to thirty-six inches. The bath-room was the major problem. A therapist suggested the pur-chase of a lift to get Rick into the bathtub. If Rick had already invented the tub-slide shower chair, the entire bath-room would have been accessible to him, but that invention was eight years down the road.

The therapists also toured the outside of the house and the basement. They discussed building a wooden ramp to gain wheelchair access to the house. To our dismay we figured that the ramp would have to be about thirty-five feet long. That was something we had to think about. There had to be an easier solution.

Eventually we returned to Boston in our new Chevrolet Impala sedan. Our previous station wagon was not the best type of vehicle on which to install a lift on the roof. This sedan had wider doors and a smooth roof that served our purpose better. We purchased a Hoyer lift to transfer him in and out of the car. In order to use the lift a portion of it had to be secured to the roof of the car and other parts were manually attached as needed to transfer him.

Now we felt we were ready for the next chapter in Rick's recovery.

CHAPTER EIGHT

A TRIP TO THE CAPE

One memorable Friday afternoon Rick was prepared for his first long weekend at our summer home. His urine output was bloody, but the doctor gave him permission for a home visit anyway, and Rick was pleased that Bonnie had joined us. We helped Rick into his wheelchair, packed his suit case, gathered his medication, extra catheters (my husband had been taught how to insert the catheter and irrigate it), irrigating set, his drinking container, and his one-and-half-pound exercising weights. I thought it would be wise to somehow tie Rick into his seat while we drove. Although the safety belt could be used, it was not enough to hold Rick upright, in case of an accident. The therapist gave us an ace bandage to slip under the seat and over his shoulders and finally off we went.

We headed toward our home in Harwich on Cape Cod, a long, busy one-hundred-mile ride. We had no trouble getting Rick into the house. We had learned how to transfer him with his previous visit to our other home, and we were happy and eager to arrive at the Cape, Rick's favorite place.

The Cape house was located on a quiet side street. It was surrounded by conservation land with a fourteen-mile bike trail. In the fall when the foliage was gone you could see the bikers from our front window. The house was a modest split-level three-bedroom ranch. The front door opened into a huge cathedral ceiling living room with a red brick raised hearth floor-to-ceiling fireplace. This room was what attracted us to the house. Here we often lit a fire and sat with a hot bowl of popcorn to watch the fire glow. On rainy days you could hear the sound of rain on the roof. A large bay window was located on one side of the room giving it an airy look—something akin to a ski lodge. It was a spot Rick and our family always enjoyed. The three bedrooms were on the farthest end of the house. Here the quiet was unbroken even by the television in the living room.

The bedroom furniture had to be rearranged to make room for Rick's wheelchair. The twin beds were pushed together allowing ample room for his care. In bed he was propped on his side with pillows so later in the night one of us could merely pull out the pillows allowing his position to be easily changed. We placed his drinking container on a little table next to him and put the drinking tube in his mouth. He was able to sip water without help using this gadget.

We all planned to sleep late in the morning especially Rick who needed his rest. However, I rose early to give Rick his medications. When I entered the room, he appeared half asleep. He opened his mouth and I dropped the pills on his tongue. He took a sip of water and went right back to sleep. Three hours later it was time to get up.

The facilities at the Cape house could not accommodate Rick for a shower or tub bath; so I had to give him a bed-bath. We decided a quick sponge bath would be sufficient. I washed his back thoroughly and rubbed it with alcohol, I connected the urinary leg bag to his catheter and dressed him. Rick had to be moved gradually to a sitting position so that he would not get dizzy. I sat him up in his bed for five minutes before I transferred him to his wheelchair to go to the breakfast table. The wheelchair arms did not fit under the table, but we easily solved that problem. My husband placed a piece of plywood on the arms of the chair. It worked well. Rick—grinning from ear to ear—thoroughly enjoyed his sausage and eggs breakfast especially prepared by Bonnie.

In the afternoon, Rick was determined to do his exercises. My husband, Bonnie and I lifted him out of the wheelchair and placed him gently on a mat on the living room floor. I tied a one-and-a-half pound weight to his wrist. Then he worked strenuously to get his shoulders moving and his elbow bending back and forth. It was very sad to watch. He was trying so hard that the terrible stress showed on his face, but he could manage very little movement. Next came the exercises on his legs. The effort he made was unbelievable. He was so tired after a short time; he actually fell asleep on the mat.

The weather was mild and so we planned to grill steaks for supper. We ate in the living room in front of the beautiful fire burning in the fireplace. After supper Rick wanted to sit on the couch, to feel normal I supposed. Obviously, he had not fully accepted the wheelchair. We transferred him to the couch and Bonnie nestled close to him. They watched television together while my husband and I went to bed to give them some privacy. When it was time to get Rick into bed for the night, Bonnie rapped on our bedroom door and I put him to bed. I covered him with a sheet and blanket, because he was still not able to pull the covers up on to himself. I hooked up his catheter to the bedside drainage bottle on the floor, put the water gadget to his mouth, gave him his evening medicines and he was settled for the night.

I went to bed and fell sound asleep. Shortly, it seemed, I heard in the background a call for "Dad, Dad." Out of curiosity, I got up to check on Rick. He had managed to raise one arm and could not lower it. He was in great pain. He had been trying to wake some one for an hour. A bell eventually was tied to his wrist to call us. I changed his position and went back to bed. During the night I checked on him periodically. Once he was hot and I removed his blanket. Another time he was cold and I replaced it. I did not get much sleep.

The morning was the usual routine, bed-bath, hair shampoo, medicines, and out of bed into the wheelchair. This weekend went by much too quickly and it was time to pack all his supplies and head back to the hospital.

We arrived at the hospital in time for supper, but Rick wasn't hungry. In fact, he felt sick. His nose was stuffed up and he had signs of a cold. The nurses took his temperature and it was elevated. The nurses put him to bed early. We said our good-byes and headed home. On the way home, my thoughts were with my son. Another set back. The cold would probably last a week and once again he would lose ground. I worried that the cold might develop into something more serious. I had to remind myself that other quads also had colds and soon felt better and that would be the case with Rick.

The next day Rick looked the same, but he was trying to make the best of things in spite of his stuffy nose and general overall misery. He showed me his latest accomplishment with great pride. He had addressed an envelope to his girlfriend in his own handwriting. The writing looked like a first grader's printing. All the letters were large with irregular spaces and sizes. It was done with a pencil taped to his thumb. He was able to do this using his left shoulder muscles. It was amazing. His fingers, hands, and forearms were paralyzed and were of no use to him, but yet he used the muscles left in his upper arms to do his eating and writing.

❦   ❦   ❦

Another home visit weekend had arrived. This time we drove Rick to Worcester. The trip was only a forty-five minute drive, much shorter than the Cape trip. I planned a Saturday night party in our basement for all his neighbor-hood friends—the boys who visited him frequently in the hospital. About a dozen of them arrived early that evening. They helped me wheel Rick outdoors around the rear of the house to the basement door. The basement is an attractive area, a finished playroom with soft chairs and a television, which had often been enjoyed by our children and their friends. The boys like being away from parents upstairs. I served the gang homemade pizzas and soft drinks. The music was loud and the laughter and talk were even louder. The party was a great success. The next-door neighbors probably heard the music and laughter but this was one time I certain-ly did not worry about it. Around midnight the boys wheeled Rick back upstairs. He had had a wonderful time. Later the next day, when the neighbors heard he was home, they dropped in to see him. He was well known in the neighborhood because as a young fellow he was the paperboy for many years.

When Rick was home, I usually prepared his favorite meals. Every meal was served with a huge tossed salad containing cherry tomatoes and black olives. His greatest challenge was piercing the tomatoes and olives with his fork. With his usual determination he conquered them and savored every last tomato and olive. Again I felt tempted to help him but I knew he would get angry with me.

"I'll get it, let me be," was his usual reaction.

Like any eighteen-year-old Rick liked to keep moving. He was not happy sitting at home with Mom and Dad. One day Bonnie decided to get him into the car and take him for a ride. They were gone for a few hours. Before they left I told them to toot the horn when they returned, so we could move him from the car to the wheelchair. When I heard the horn, I went out to the car. There was Rick with a triumphant smile on his face and a bouquet of red carnations wrapped in green tissue paper, held as best as he could manage in his paralyzed hands. I was so touched by the whole thing I had a tough time holding back my tears.

On Halloween weekend, Gina carved out a pumpkin for her brother. Gina is artistic, so the completed job looked like a work of art. The eyes and a smiling mouth were beautifully carved. We dried and salted the inner seeds, and I shelled each seed and placed them into Rick's mouth one at a time. I felt as though I understood how a mother bird feels feeding her young chick.

It now became routine to bring Rick home each weekend. We adjusted to packing up all his paraphernalia, and I tried to plan activities to make his visit home fun. One week my husband bought him a headset for the telephone, so he could talk and listen without holding on to anything. It was similar to that operators used. The gadget assembly caused some confusion and certainly Rick's intuitive instructions were essential. My husband had only to hold the screwdriver. Rick did all the inventive work.

We had also bought him a new headset for the stereo tape player, which Rick proudly showed his friends. I was glad that he enjoyed listening to all his favorite music. But I was glad for other reasons too. Music has the ability to reduce muscle tension. It regulates stress-related hormones and strengthens the immune system. The exhilaration people experience when listening to music is a result of endorphins being released. It is similar to what runners experience. Endorphins are released, pleasure is experienced, and stress is reduced. The result is a feeling of well being.

Friends and neighbors continued to come to visit Rick, often bringing food and gifts. Even the City Manager of Worcester came to visit making him feel important. As with everyone the manager was extremely impressed with Rick's attitude and sunny disposition. Rick was very talkative, as usual, when the manager arrived. Rick explained how conferences were held in the hospital with patients and staff, so that patients could bring to the forefront conditions that were not good and so that conditions could be improved. Often the paraplegics had more complaints then the quadriplegics. Rick found this puzzling. The manager was impressed with Rick's way of thinking.

❧   ❧   ❧

Time was coming close for Rick's discharge from the hospital. He had his own wheelchair, and our home had been assessed for renovations. As far as the staff was concerned his rehabilitation was complete. So his next move was to go home and face the big world with challenges that at times might seem insurmountable and at times overwhelming.

And prayer was my only consolation.

O, God, why has this happened to Rick?
O, God, why is this happening to me?
O, God, help me.

CHAPTER NINE

COMING HOME AND LEAVING HOME

It had been five months since Rick's accident and the doctors at the University Hospital in Boston felt he had progressed enough to be discharged. It was a cold December day, when Tony and I drove to Boston to pick up my son. We were ecstatic to see this day arrive. The car was nicely equipped with the Hoyer lift for transferring Rick. The lift worked well and Rick did not seem to be concerned about the safety of it. He had a swing-type cushion underneath him and he would sway a little unnervingly in mid air as he was moved into position to be transferred in or out of the car.

We arrived home with several items that were suggested by the therapists to make his life easier. The electric wheelchair was a blessing for he no longer had to struggle to maneuver the manual wheelchair. A commode chair was delivered which made part of his daily care easier. The slide board was also a great help for transferring him. His splint for feeding was an absolute necessity because he could not eat without it. We simply bent our silverware into a right angle which made it possible for Rick to feed himself. It seemed that almost all my silverware was bent into a right angle. Each member of the family grabbed a spoon or fork and bent it for Rick. I finally had to tell them to stop bending the silverware. We had more than enough.

The doctors prescribed several pills which Rick had to take four times a day. Most of the pills were to prevent a urinary tract infection. There was also a tranquilizer to help him relax. This type of injury causes spasms especially in the legs. At times Rick's legs actually fell off the wheelchair footrest and had to be placed back on them.

Rick was extremely happy to get home. No more unwelcome early awakening by the nurses to take his temperature and start his care. He could finally sleep late. Our family was relieved of all that traveling to and from hospitals. As a family we could now sit together for our meals and try to live a more normal life. Naturally we were well aware of the many adjustments we would have to make.

Rick was discharged on December nineteenth. To help elevate his spirits we flew the American flag at our front door and hung a "Welcome Home" sign that covered the entire new entrance that was made especially for him. He smiled with pleasure, but I knew he was frightened and sad. I could see it in his eyes. I could almost feel the guilt, as if he was thinking, "How could I have done this to my family?"

The burden of most of his care would mostly be placed on me. I was retired from my nursing career and available while other members of our family carried on with their lives, with work and school. Rick's care in the hospital was constant for twenty-four hours a day. Sometimes two or three nurses cared for him at one time. I was worried. How was I going to handle that? As for Rick, he loved me dearly and it hurt him to think what he had done to my life. He felt he must regain some independence to relieve me of this burden. He lost the life he knew and I lost the son I knew. I had fear also. It was like taking my child and beginning all over again. We both needed God's help to go on.

To me, the grief I experienced with this loss, was like the grief I had experienced when loved ones died. As written in Elizabeth Kubler-Ross's book *On Death and Dying* one may experience five phases of grief: denial, anger, bargaining, depression, and acceptance. I went through all the phases except anger. Never once did I blame God. I felt it was Rick's destiny and part of God's plan. God had his reasons for not having Rick drown. Rick survived because God had work for him to do. Although I did not show my anger over this tragedy, the most devastating phase of all was my severe depression, which lasted many years. The last phase is acceptance, a phase I presently have and a compelling reason for writing this book.

✤   ✤   ✤

By the time Rick was discharged, the changes that the therapist recommended had been made to the bathroom, including the installation of a lift which allowed Rick to be lowered into the bathtub. The lift did not work well. Rick could not hold himself erect and kept sliding down into the water. Therefore, it was of primary importance to replace the bathtub with a wheel in shower. Tony, a great handy man, quickly went to work and proceeded to remove the bathtub by using a sledgehammer. He gleefully tossed the pieces out the bathroom window. He had the assistance of a tile man to install a tile floor pitched toward a drain in the middle of the floor for the water run off. Tony had also done the carpentry work to widen the doors to the bathroom and to Rick's bedroom.

To avoid building a thirty-foot ramp leading to the house, Tony cut a new door opening from the garage directly into the kitchen. We bought an electric operated wheel-a-vator or lift that was set up in the garage. Now the problem of getting into the house and the bathroom was solved.

When Rick arrived home, he was actually somewhat uneasy. Each day at the hospital was filled with activities. There were work outs in the rec room. Patients traveled around the hospital trying to push their wheelchairs. The patients were brought out of the hospital to attend auto shows and even went bowling. The staff made Rick's stay very enjoyable. But now he was home. What could be done to keep him occupied? We never saw Rick cry since he was hurt. He looked sad many days but soon snapped out of it. His attitude made our adjustments that much easier.

His daily routine—getting him out of bed, giving him his bath and shampoo and getting him dressed—took most of the morning. My husband or I gave him this morning care. At night we took turns getting up and turning him. Although we placed an air mattress on his bed, we still had to turn him every two hours. After a month of this routine, on the advice of our doctor, we decided it would be more beneficial to have a nurse come daily, so I could maintain my role as his mother rather than his nurse.

The visiting nurse came Monday through Friday but did not come on Saturday or Sunday or stormy days. I filled in on these days. This routine worked very well. Although I was about 110 pounds and Rick 140 pounds, I was able to lift him without a problem. I followed his instructions. I leaned over, locked my forearms under his armpits and hooked him toward me, as if lifting a large log from underneath. Then I straightened up, hoisting him as I rose making a pivot with my legs.

The days spent at home were filled with visiting friends and relatives. His high school classmates came four and five at a time. The house was humming with lots of people and Rick thrived on all the attention. Many hours were spent playing table games such as Scrabble and chess. Although Rick could not place any of the game pieces, he told his opponent where to move them. When he played cards, we put the cover of a shoe box under the bottom of the box and slipped the cards between the cover and the bottom of the box. This worked out fine. There were so many little problems that arose that needed a mechanical mind to solve them. We had one—Rick's.

✾ ✾ ✾

But not everything was rosy. We had our down moments. One morning while I was giving Rick his morning care, he became very frustrated. He was giving me instructions and I was not following them. And in this frustrating moment he must have felt all the frustration of his situation, and he began to cry. It was the first—and only— time I saw him cry, and I, too, began to cry. And we cried and cried and cried.

As I look back on it, I guess I would call it a good cry. It was a kind of catharsis. We needed to get it out of our systems, and we did.

❦   ❦   ❦

Rick was getting stronger each day and as expected he became bored. He decided to enroll in Worcester's Quinsigamond Community College for the spring semester. How were we to get him there? At first my husband used his utility trailer to transport the wheelchair and placed Rick in his car, but this was difficult and slow. Later we hired a wheelchair accessible van. This continued for one semester. Then we decided to purchase our own van, had it customized, and brought Rick to the college ourselves. At college, Rick elected mostly business courses such as business law and bookkeeping. He used a tape recorder for lectures and received help from other students. He did well. His first report card showed good grades. It was a surprise to us. Can it be, that there had been a miracle and our son had finally become a serious student?

❦   ❦   ❦

I found this essay in an old chest stored in my basement. It was written by Rick as an English assignment in his first year at Quinsigamond Community College. He was nineteen years old.

From Independence to Dependence

June second, 1973 was the best day of my life, for that day I graduated from high school. I was finally through with St. John's, suit coats and ties. I had a job lined up for me which I had wanted since I was fifteen years old. That job was to be a lifeguard for the city of Worcester.

Two days later I was admitted to the hospital for a minor operation on my right knee. I was supposed to be in the hospital for four days, and on crutches for a week after that, which was fine with me because most of the pools in the city did not open until a month later, but due to complications, things did not work out as planned and I was in and out of the hospital until the beginning of July. My job had already started, but my brother was a lifeguard, so he was able to keep the position open till I was recovered enough to work. I worked four days the first week, taking Friday off so that I could go to the Cape on a long weekend with my girlfriend. For the first time, I could do whatever I wanted; go wherever I wanted and come back whenever I wanted. I finally felt completely independent and it was a great feeling. Even though the weekend passed quickly, the feeling of independence stayed. I thought it was here for good.

Monday morning I had to be at work at ten o'clock. I woke up at nine and since I had my own car, I could sit down to have a leisurely breakfast and drive to work. It was July sixteen and just about the most beautiful day you could ask for. The temperature was about eighty-five to ninety degrees, the sun was shining and there was not a cloud in the sky. As a lifeguard, whenever you get hot you could just take a dip in the pool to cool off. It got to be about noontime and I decided to give my girlfriend a call. While I was talking, I noticed that my lunch, in the corner on the ground, was getting attacked by ants. I cut the call short so that I could get to my lunch before the ants did. To this day I do not know if I ate my lunch, but I do know that I decided to do what I was getting paid for, so I climbed up in my lifeguard chair and watched the kids swim. I started to get hot and thought I should dive in the water and cool off but I could not decide whether I should dive off the platform, or jump off the side of the pool. You can probably guess, I chose the wrong one of the two. I dove off the platform arching my back since the dive was a shallow one and trying to protect my knee, but I hit the water face first and snapped my neck. I was conscious in the water for a short time but I could hold my breath long enough for someone to pull me out.

When I woke up a day and a half later, I realized that the independence I had discovered was gone. In fact, a machine was breathing for me and I was unable to move any part of my body. I did not realize how dependent I was until I got home from the hospital. There, everyone else was in about the same situation as I was in.

I came home in the middle of December and it was too cold to go outside so I was stuck in the house. It got to be depressing staying in the house all the time.

It's hard to get over the feeling of helplessness. I have to be put into bed and taken out of it. Someone has to wash and dress me, put the television on and change the channels for me. If I want a drink of water someone has to get it for me. I can feed myself, but someone has to put an attachment on my hand so that I can hold a fork, and cut up my food for me.

It's impossible for me to state all the ways I am dependent upon others but I tried to keep it short. Anyway, I think I've said enough to make it clear that my life has changed drastically since my accident. One of these days I will get my independence back because I'm sure they will find a cure for my injury.

The teacher's comments read:

Richard, this is well done and admirably controlled in it's description of the major moments with no artificial drama, your head makes others at ease, and your courage is quiet and strong.

✽   ✽   ✽

Although Rick had been discharged from the hospital, he still had several medical problems. In February, two months after his discharge, he was readmitted to the University Hospital in Boston with a severe urinary tract infection. He remained hospitalized for ten long weeks. Several months later, he was hospitalized again for a severe cold. It was discouraging. He was unable to blow his nose or cough up any mucous. We found pushing up on his diaphragm helped him to expectorate. There was a constant fear of pneumonia, and he remained hospitalized for four days. Three months later again he was readmitted to the University Hospital with severe diarrhea brought on by some of his medications. This stay was ten days. Urinary tract infections persisted and caused him to have a fever and cloudy urine. Eventually we were able to treat them without going into the hospital. Each year for the next five years, he was admitted to the University Hospital for his routine check-up. He was fortunate, that excellent nursing care avoided bedsores, which would have meant more hospitalization.

❧ ❧ ❧

Springtime arrived, and it was the beginning of good weather and better health for Rick. He wanted to keep moving, not sit at home. We bought him a commuter or a scooter operated by battery for outdoor use. It was similar to a golf cart but had one seat instead of two. It was too large to be brought inside the home, so we had to wheel Rick outside and transfer him into the scooter. Merrily, off he went usually down to the corner store. Here his buddies gathered to "chew the fat." This meant he traveled down hill, across the state highway and across another main road to get to the corner less than a mile away. He was fearless and loved this new toy. One day he was traveling too fast and bumped into the curbing, in doing so he tipped forward. The batteries were located under the rear and to get to them you had to raise the seat. The jolt that occurred popped the rear of the commuter up, leaving Rick hanging in mid air. He was strapped in, so he did not fall out. He was now stuck in this position unable to move. This was a humbling, helpless and perhaps somewhat comical situation. Fortunately, the windows were open in several nearby homes, so his cry for help was heard. A young man came out, set him straight and off he went as if nothing happened. His main concern was the condition of the scooter. Had his favorite toy been damaged?

At this time Rick and Bonnie decided to break-up. She was involved with her nursing career and studying and had less free time for Rick. Of course, Rick was not the boy she used to know and share activities with such as dancing. They both came to an agreement not to see one another anymore. I expected Rick to show a great deal of sadness about their separation, but he didn't seem unhappy. He is a survivor.

Rick spent most of the summer on his commuter. His friends gathered at the corner each evening and Rick was there to join them. His friends were very loyal to him; they drew closer and circled wagons of love around him. They filled his evenings by being together. One Saturday evening they picked him up to take him out to a party at a friend's house. They gathered together all of their strength to carry him and his chair—all of 400 pounds—to his friends' apartment located on the second floor. The friends brought Rick home after midnight that night. I took one look at Rick and knew he had had too much to drink. He was so drunk he could not hold his head up. Tony and I got him into bed for the night as we usually did. We were, of course, disappointed to see him in this condition. However, we realized perhaps he needed to blow off steam and live it up a little. We said nothing at the time. Later I scolded him.

"Your head is the only good thing you have, and if you want to do that to it, it will be up to you."

After this incident, I never saw Rick drunk again.

❧   ❧   ❧

In May 1974, my son Bob was graduating from the University of Bridgeport in Connecticut and, of course, Tony and I wanted to attend. It meant that Rick would be left alone for a while. We talked it over with him and he insisted that we go. He asked some of his friends to visit with him. Rick was now able to make telephone calls himself, using a pencil in his mouth to press the numbers and a splint to slide over his hand to pick up the receiver. Being able to use the telephone was of enormous importance for his safety. We knew he would be fine. When we arrived home, I noticed Rick had two blisters on his left index and middle fingers. Evidently he was smoking with his friends and unknowingly burnt his fingers. This can easily happen to anyone who has no feeling in his extremities.

❧   ❧   ❧

For Rick, life could be an adventure. One day when my husband and I returned from shopping, Rick was nowhere to be found. We looked in the only three rooms he could enter, the bathroom, the living room and the bed room. We looked up and down the street and in the front and backyard, but no Rick. We finally found Rick in his wheelchair stuck in the mud between groups of evergreens in our backyard. Not being able to use the commuter because we were not at home, he had been able to get himself out of the house in his wheel-chair. To accomplish this he needed only wheel himself on the wheel-a-vator and lower himself using a switch on the side. He only ran into difficulty when he tried to navigate the yard on this spring day and found to his dismay that the wheels on his wheelchair sunk in the muddy ground.

"What in the world are you doing?" I asked in exaspera-tion. We had been frightened.

"Just studying evergreens," he said smiling.

He discovered that his wheelchair was a terrible chariot on muddy terrain.

      ✤   ✤   ✤

One evening during his usual corner get together Rick became acquainted with a lovely girl, Lori. She lived in an apartment above the corner store. She was the same age as Rick and divorced with a year-old daughter, Zoe. She had straight blonde hair, used no make-up, wore jeans most of the time and ate mostly organic food. She broke away from her short-lived and unhappy marriage and courageously went off on her own with her infant daughter. At the time we had the impression her domestic problem must have been extremely serious to leave.

Lori was sad and lonely when she first met Rick. Rick was determined to change that and make her life satisfying and fun.

Ironically Rick was able to enter Lori's apartment without any trouble. The building was built into a hill so the door leading to her second-floor apartment was at ground level. When the weather changed to cold and wintry, Rick was not able to use his commuter only his wheelchair. Each evening Rick left the house and went to spend the evening with Lori. They enjoyed each other's company. Most of his friends were now attending college so the gang was no longer around. Every evening, Lori would call us to let us know when Rick was on his way home. She made sure he was well protected from the cold and wrapped his legs in blankets. She realized that Rick could not feel the cold and could easily become frostbitten. This continued for the entire winter.

One stormy night a light covering of snow had fallen and Rick had not returned home. He was half way home when the circuit breaker on his electric wheelchair popped off and left him without power. He was stranded in the middle of the street. My husband and son Bob went out to find him, and then they had to face the problem of pushing the 400 pound wheelchair up a snowy hill. The boys did some quick thinking. Tony drove the car while Bob sat on the hood guiding the wheelchair, as the car slowly pushed the chair up the hill. Rick arrived safely home laughing over the incident. Sure, he just had to sit there comfortably while others rescued him in the cold.

In the spring Lori decided to move from her apartment over the store. She found another about 100 yards from our home. Unfortunately Rick was unable to enter this new second floor apartment, so Lori and her daughter now came to see Rick instead. When the nurses did not come to care for Rick on weekends, holidays and stormy days, Lori took over his care. She learned how to handle Rick without any problem. She seemed to be a born nurse. Meanwhile, I entertained Zoe in my kitchen making homemade cookies. Zoe enjoyed getting her hands in the flour and rolling out cookies with me. Rick and Lori's relationship blossomed.

In 1975, two years after his injury, Rick informed us that he, Lori and Zoe would like to live on Cape Cod. This meant more renovations. Our Cape home was a split-level ranch with the garage located underneath the bedroom area. It wasn't long before the entire lower level became Rick's apartment. It was sixty-five feet long, the length of the house, with plenty of room for maneuvering a wheelchair. It was decorated in a masculine rustic motif. The ceiling had dark stained beams and the walls were white stucco. The full-length windows made the apartment bright. The floor was covered with a brick linoleum pattern. A wheel-in-shower was built making daily showers easier. The apartment was equipped with a complete kitchen including a disposal, dishwasher, microwave oven and a frost-free refrigerator. The former garage was divided in half. The front was the laundry room and the rear part became a cozy bedroom for Zoe. With the exception of the plumbing, heating and electricity, Tony did the entire renovation.

When Lori first lived with Rick she had issues with her family. There seemed to be some anger left over from her childhood. Rick discussed the importance of family with her. She absorbed his insight and soon her mother, sisters and brother were frequent visitors at their Harwich apartment.

Rick's decision to move to the Cape was a good one. Worcester was no longer a place where there were pleasant memories. His friends were away at college. He endured his tragic accident and the break-up with his girlfriend. He needed to get away from his parents. He needed a change and wanted to start a new life. If this change was going to bring him happiness we were all for it.

CHAPTER TEN

THE MOVE TO CAPE COD

In the spring of 1975 Rick moved into his new apartment on Herring Run Road in Harwich, Massachusetts. Along with him came his entourage—Lori, his girlfriend and her two-year-old daughter, Zoe.

Zoe was a cute little girl who looked just like her mother with a light complexion and straight blond hair. They arrived with bits and pieces from Lori's apartment such as Zoe's youth bed and other personal furnishings. The apartment needed to be furnished. The first thing they bought was a queen size waterbed, a necessity that not only kept Rick's skin healthy but also eliminated the need to turn him as frequently.

His spacious bedroom was furnished with two dressers I had found in an antique shop. One was a curly maple chest with a mirror and the other was a maple chest of drawers. There was ample room around the bed for his wheelchair to be maneuvered. Off the bedroom were two doors, one led to the wheel-in-shower room, the other to the living room. In the bedroom, there were plenty of built-in cabinets to store extra pillows, blankets and space for his commode chair. For the living room he selected a soft tweed convertible sofa available for overnight guests.

Rick admired antiques and had started a collection. I was given the tough job of roaming the shops looking for treasures. I found a beautiful large beveled mirror, a mahogany rocker, an old treadle sewing machine and several old chairs, which he used in his living room. A round table high enough to accommodate his wheelchair, and three chairs were arranged in the living area which afforded a grand view through the full-length windows of the outdoors. The small kitchen was efficiently equipped with all appliances. Although the interior of the apartment was comfortable for this little family, several changes would have to be made. The one car concrete driveway was no longer adequate for the wheelchair accessible van. My husband got to work and added six feet to the width. He graded it, ordered the cement and proceeded to spread it. While working with my brothers' construction company Tony had learned this sort of work. His time and effort were all that he needed to complete the job.

Rick's friends visited the Cape often and needed a place to socialize and have cookouts. On the west side of the house my husband laid red bricks into sand to make a large patio. He furnished it with patio furniture, lounge chairs and an umbrella. This was a wonderful addition. Everyone enjoyed eating outdoors. It's a great place to sit, have a cold drink and chat with friends. The terrain leading to the rear of the house was not wheelchair accessible, so Tony once again did some work. He installed a four-foot red brick walkway leading to the rear deck and at the same time cut an opening in the deck so we could install another wheel-a-vator. Now it was possible for Rick to get onto the deck and into our upstairs living area. The major construction and renovations were now complete.

The fall season was approaching and Rick wanted to continue his education at Cape Cod Community College known on the Cape as "The 4 C's." Before he enrolled, my husband and I visited the campus in Hyannis. To our chagrin we found numerous hills and steps not conducive to wheelchair travel. When we got home, we told Rick all about it.

"I'll manage somehow. I want to attend," he replied.

Rick transferred his credits from Quinsigamond Community College and he started class in the fall semester.

He was the first wheelchair student to attend the college. It was not easy for him to do so. He had to ask for help going up stairs, opening doors and toughest of all, asking to have his urinary leg bag emptied. Lori, who drove the van, transported him to and from the college.

The visiting nurses association was no longer caring for Rick. He made arrangements through a nurse's registry for daily nurses. He had a difficult time. Some nurses were unable to lift him and each day he had a different caregiver. It was frustrating for Rick to have to repeat the same instructions over and over again.

Lori put him to bed at night. She also gave him his morning medicine before the nurses arrived. It seemed he was not getting sick as often since he moved to the Cape. Eventually Lori weaned him off all his medications. She was preparing good wholesome nourishing food to replace them.

There was space next to the patio for a small vegetable garden. Lori planted tomatoes, green beans, peppers, squash and even some red raspberry bushes. Rick got lots of enjoyment watching the garden grow as well as eating the fresh produce for his meals.

Of course, their little family would not be complete without a dog. They purchased a purebred collie puppy and named him "Beau Jay." How Rick loved that dog. Soon they also got a cat. The two animals got along well. When the dog was matured enough, Rick secured the leash to his wheelchair and walked the dog around the neighborhood.

✤   ✤   ✤

At first after Lori moved into her new apartment, Zoe was not herself. She showed signs of jealousy. She wanted her mother's full attention and did not appreciate sharing her with Rick. This rebellion disappeared once Zoe was enrolled in a preschool program, which she loved. Rick and Zoe then got along famously. He often gave Zoe rides on his wheelchair. She stood on his feet with her back toward him, while he traveled as fast as the chair would go—about five miles an hour. She giggled all the while enjoying every minute of it. She was too young to realize that Lori and Rick were sharing the same bed.

Many people are understandably curious how such injured people make love. I have never asked Rick, but articles that I have read state: a substantial number, though not an overwhelming proportion of spinal cord injured will have essentially normal sexual functioning. Another group will have the ability to perform sexually but will not experience orgasm or ejaculate. A third group will be unable to do anything as far as genital sexuality is concerned; but this does not mean that sex is a dead issue. I have no idea in which category Rick falls and I do not care to know. It is a personal matter.

✼   ✼   ✼

Rick was always a great sun lover. During the summer months, after his morning shower, he was stripped to the waist, wheeled himself outdoors and parked on the sunny driveway to relax and bask in the sun. He attracted the children in the neighborhood like a magnet. They were always around him asking questions about his injury. What had happened to him and why couldn't he walk, they wanted to know. He loved them all.

The painful rash on his face remained. It was very unattractive. The treatment that was prescribed did little good. After one innocent child asked him what had happened to his face, Rick was taken aback and decided to hide the rash with a full beard that he sported for several years.

The children waited for him to come outside each day. They brought him some of their technical problems such as a chain falling off a bicycle or a mother's broken toaster. He gave them specific directions and under his watchful eye they were able to make their own repairs.

The first birthday Rick celebrated on the Cape was his twentieth. We had the usual birthday cake and gathered to sing Happy Birthday. Zoe sang heartily and especially enjoyed the festivities. Lori bought him an extremely unique present, one perhaps everyone would not appreciate—a tarantula spider in a glass cage. Immediately they named him "Fido." It was a pet that required very little care and was interesting to watch. It was an unusual pet to say the least. Its food consisted of live crickets. Periodically it shed its outer skin. Some of the neighborhood children who saw the tarantula would say "Yek" and others would say "Neat." One child brought the spider's outer skin to his classroom for "Show and Tell." Fido made a lasting impression.

Rick focused on things he could see, hear, taste and smell—the only senses he could use. He kept himself busy with various occupations to take his mind off his disability. He frequently bought fresh colorful flowers for his table to capture their scent. He also bought a camera to take pictures of the local colorful birds. The camera was mounted on a tripod which was then fastened to Rick's wheelchair. Rick would snap the picture by pressing the button with a pencil in his mouth. Rick also took great pleasure in a huge fish aquarium in his apartment with many colorful tropical fish.

Rick was determined that this injury would not get him down. His suffering had caused him to look at life differently than the average person. He sees a bluer sky and a prettier flower, he hears sweeter music and tastes the most delicious meals. Rick doesn't tolerate petty situations. If someone has difficulty seeing such a young, handsome boy in a wheelchair his response is apt be that it's his or her problem.

✾ ✾ ✾

When Rick started his education in the fall, he selected business courses and several computer courses. He also enrolled in a child psychology course. Living with a three-year-old he wanted to know more about children and their behavior. It took him five years to graduate with an associate's degree in business administration.

After graduation I planned a party in our home for him. There were so many guests in one room that my husband was concerned that the floor might collapse. I had a huge feast with, of course, plenty of delicious food—after all I am an Italian mother. My family came in from Worcester and all the neighbors and his loyal friends were there. Zoe, now eight years old, and taking violin lessons, stood in the center of the living room to entertain the group with a violin solo. The audience applauded with big smiles and Lori beamed with pride.

Soon after his graduation, Rick called me in Worcester. From the tone of his voice, I could sense his excitement. The college wanted him to stay on and monitor the computer lab for a few hours every evening. This gave him a big boost. He had the satisfaction of knowing he was needed and would be helpful to other students.

Rick had been well liked in college and had made several friends. A few years later in the curriculum guide catalog, they photographed him seated at his computer. He worked in the South building. A convenient handicap parking space was close by. The computer lab was on the ground floor, but Rick knew the entire South Building like the palm of his hand. Sometimes, when he worked late at night, a student would ask where one could find something in the building. Rick was the right guy to ask. Although he had never been on the second floor, he knew exactly where everything was located. He knew the location of each secretary on the second floor, and where to find such things as a copying machine or a microwave.

Many years later an elevator was finally installed. Rick took the elevator, rolled onto the floor and heads turned as he wheeled down the corridor. People cheered and called out to him. He was thrilled. He had meant to bring flowers to the secretaries up there but never got around to it.

❦   ❦   ❦

My husband was employed by the city as a district fire chief; so we were not able to be on the Cape full time. Each time we arrived, I invited Rick's little family upstairs for dinner. They enjoyed my old fashioned homemade cooking. Lori, Rick and Zoe got along well and appeared very happy. We liked Lori and often admired her for all the things she did for my son. She was like an angel sent to us from heaven. She gave me a nice compliment one day saying, "I wish you were my mother."

They kept themselves busy so I had to call Rick in advance to be sure he would be home to join us for dinner. They often went to the movies, saw plays and went out to dinner.

❀   ❀   ❀

Rick continued to have trouble finding nurses to care for him in the morning. Finally a nurse came who was dynamic, trustworthy, kind, knowledgeable and most important was available daily. Her name was Denny. She also worked at the Spaulding Rehabilitation Hospital in Boston. She spent four hours with Rick in the early morning and then commuted to Boston. Denny still comes to care for Rick today. She surely is a heavenly angel.

❀   ❀   ❀

I left no leaf unturned in trying to find a treatment that would restore Rick's mobility. I even wrote to the U.S. Embassy in Russia. I had read a newspaper article, which said the Russians were having great success in treating spinal cord injuries. After some research, however, I discovered that their treatment was no different than ours. I also attended a spinal cord injury convention in Boston to learn as much as possible about Rick's injury. What I did learn at the convention, was that a young boy in the same condition as my son was able to drive his wheelchair accessible van. I could not wait to get home to tell Rick. I was so excited. I did not have to tell him that he could do it too. He was immediately convinced. We already had the van; it just had to be modified to accommodate Rick's driving. It took many visits to a special company to accomplish this. He was tested at the Braintree Rehab for his vision, coordination and reflexes. All were good and he was ready to go. He passed the driving test the first time without any trouble. He received his Massachusetts driver's license five years after his accident. The experiences that came as a result will fill another entire chapter. Obviously the freedom offered by driving the van opened all sorts of new possibilities.

❦   ❦   ❦

Rick's beautiful relationship with Lori lasted eight enjoyable years. One day she announced that she felt she must move on with her life. She left Rick to start college and planned a new career in nursing. When she moved out she took the dog and the cat. My son was not able to care for these animals himself. I was greatly concerned for Rick. He knew how I felt, sad and disappointed but he reassured me that he would be fine.

Rick's life was filled with activity. He worked at the college during the summer months and the neighbors would drop into his apartment just to sit and chat with him. He managed his life fairly well. Denny came daily, he went to the college in the evening, and traveled to restaurants for some of his meals. Donna, a neighbor, put him to bed at night. Donna had five little boys, and she was happy to have a part-time job. She lived behind our house, and she and Rick got along very well. She would walk through our backyard, in her nightgown and robe, to put Rick to bed. Rick wanted his life to be causal and casual it was.

Lori was gone and there was a void in Rick's life. And before long he met a young lady named Adria who was taking courses at the college. She was entirely different from Lori. She was living alone on the Cape attending school while her family lived in Randolph, Massachusetts, a town not far from Boston. She was Rick's age, with short brunette hair, small in stature and very athletic. Every time I looked at her pretty face, she reminded me of a young Katherine Hepburn.

Adria made Rick's meals, kept his clothing clean, cut his meat and helped him put on a sweater if he needed to, in short she met his needs. Rick and Adria had a lot of fun together. For instance on one of the coldest days of the winter after a huge snowstorm, Adria and Rick went north on a ski trip. They traveled to Loon Mountain in Lincoln, New Hampshire, with a group to go skiing. This was something Rick had never done. One trail was set up for the handicapped. He was placed in a big bucket sled with outrigger skis to provide balance and steering and was guided down the slope by an able bodied person on skis with a rope to hold on to the sled. Rick was well protected from the cold with hand and foot warmers. He arrived home the next day full of excitement over his new experience.

Of course Rick's household had to have a dog. When Adria moved in with Rick, they decided to get a dog. They did some research and wanted to have a purebred Rottweiler. They found a breeder in the Boston area and off they went to pick up a ten week-old female. They named her Kali. They were both serious about the dog's ability and training capabilities. Kali soon attended a Brockton training school and took part in several Rottweiler dog shows where she won first prize. Rick and Adria were members of a Rottweiler club where they were on the Ways and Means committee and were involved with a way to make money for the organization. There was a local chapter that published a newspaper that they also participated in. They had several pictures of the dog hung in the apartment as well as Rottweiler dog statues everywhere. They loved this dog and its breed. She was bred twice giving them a total of seven puppies that were quickly sold to some of their friends. Kali kept them very busy, something they both enjoyed. Along with the dog, Rick purchased a gray parrot. The entire household was very active with a dog, a gray parrot named "Ralph," a tarantula, and fish aquarium. Adria also bought a riding horse. Rick enjoyed going to the stable to watch her groom the horse and ride.

Adria was a capable, responsible individual and helped Rick a great deal. It was a comfort to know Rick was not alone especially when traveling long distances to Worcester on holidays. After Adria came into Rick's life, he quickly discovered that she had a substance abuse problem. She liked alcohol too much. There were members of her family who were also afflicted with this addiction. She loved Rick and listened to his advice and joined Alcoholics Anonymous. One day she and I sat at her dining room table and we talked about it. In nursing I had cared for several alcoholics mostly those suffering from delirium tremors or DTs, a horrible hallucinating condition that some have with withdrawal from the alcohol. I have heard by some that they saw doorknobs turn into snakes. She invited me to attend an AA meeting with her. I was delighted and eager to know what happens when these troubled people gather. We went to a large basement meeting room furnished with a large table surrounded with chairs. A separate smaller table had hot coffee for anyone to help himself or herself. There were about a dozen people there, men and women, young and old. They each took a seat around the table. The meeting started with each one stating only their first name and told exactly how long it had been since they had their last drink. I was impressed to hear the exact days, months and years. Some were very precise. For example they would respond by saying "two months and two days." Some mentioned their incarceration. Some mentioned loss of family or job. Each person told his or her heart breaking stories. The meeting lasted until all had spoken. They broke up into groups and did more talking amongst themselves. The entire meeting was an education I could not have received anywhere else. I was thankful to have been a part of it. The best part was that Adria became addiction free and a much happier person. She continues to attend meetings today.

Adria spent several years with Rick and then she too decided she must move on. Rick felt if she moved away she would come back if it was meant to be. A few months later Adria did return. She spent a total of five years with him and then she left permanently. She went back to college to finish her education. She took nursing courses and became a registered nurse. When Adria moved away, she took Kali with her and Rick fully understood he was not able to care for a dog himself.

Both girls who lived with Rick helped him, but he also helped them to find their way. In both cases they seemed to have been lost. Both girls needed guidance in their lives and apparently the association with my son helped. Rick felt no remorse and moved on with his life as he usually did.

❦   ❦   ❦

After spending thirty-four years in the Worcester Fire Department my husband retired. It meant we would have more free time to spend in our beautiful home on the Cape. But it was a mixed blessing. I was apprehensive about Rick's driving. My bedroom was above the driveway and when he went out at night, I could not fall asleep until I heard the van pull into the driveway. Many times his friends from Worcester would arrive on their motorcycles and the noise was disturbing.

Tony and I gave the situation serious thought, and we decided that we should move away so that Rick could live as independently as possible without his parents hovering over him to make sure he was well, comfortable and safe. He needed and wanted his independence.

Tony and I contacted a real estate agent who found a house about three miles away in South Dennis. It was in the process of being built and so we had the opportunity to make some changes to accommodate the wheelchair. The entry door had to be widened and moved; the portion between the living and dining area had to be removed to have an open floor plan; and the patio door leading to the deck had to be the same level as the deck. We moved into our new three-bedroom home in September 1985. There were fourteen new homes in the area where retired professionals resided. It was quiet, an atmosphere my husband and I needed. At the end of our short street was Fresh Pond, a body of water where children swam and boated. This was ideal, away from Rick but close enough to see each other frequently.

When we moved away, our upper level was rented to a lovely family, the Franklins. Kathy and Larry had two sons Jeffrey and Gregory, ten and eleven years old. I could not have picked a lovelier, kinder, more responsible family than the Franklins. Larry worked for the town and Kathy was a stay-at-home mom. Larry was also a part-time fisherman, so fish was on their menu frequently. Kathy would make enough to bring Rick a plate which he relished every time. The two boys kept Rick company. He helped with their school projects and answered their questions, and they helped him whenever needed. It was a pleasant rewarding association that lasted eight years.

But Rick was looking for new horizons. His friend Mike, a builder, often sat with Rick in his living room discussing real estate. This inspired Rick to start thinking about real estate for himself. It was 1990 and he had spent fifteen years in the lower level of our home. He wanted to move on.

Rick at six months (top left), Rick and Bonnie before Rick's Senior Prom (top right), Rick's high school graduation picture (left), and Rick with his first wheelchair accessible van.

At top: Rick, center bottom, with (clockwise):
Gilda, Tony, Bob, and Gina.
Denny, Rick's nurse, with Rick on vacation (bottom).

At top: Rick and friends on a ski trip to Loon Mountain in 1993.
Rick skiing (bottom).

Rick scuba diving with instructors in Mexico (top).
Rick in his new kitchen (bottom).

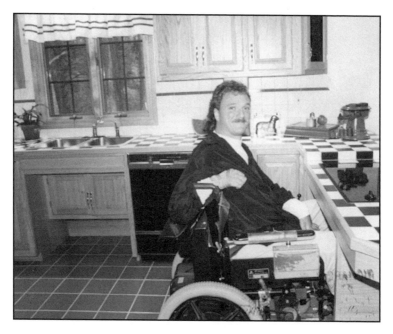

The kitchen Rick designed for his new home (top).
A view of the rear of the house (bottom).

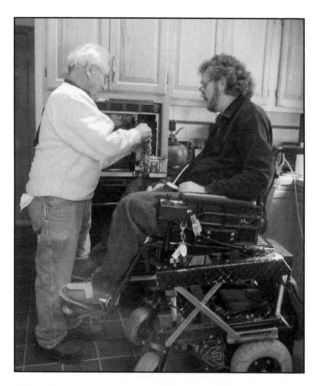

Tony fixes the microwave while Rick coaches from his
elevated wheelchair (top).

Rick and Julie all decked out for Halloween (bottom).

Julie, Jessica, and Rick as seen on their Christmas card in 2002 (top).
Tony oversees the hamburgers at the annual Pig Roast (bottom).

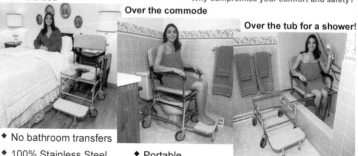

Above is an ad that features Rick's products.
It is routinely run in handicap magazines.

CHAPTER ELEVEN

THE VAN AND ITS ADVENTURES

Many people watching Rick drive away in his wheelchair in his van have a look of utter amazement on their faces. He is able to use the limited movements in his arms to the fullest. His shoulder muscles and his biceps (the upper outer arm muscles) work together enabling him to use his arms for driving. Rick does not have a problem with the upward movement but without his triceps (the lower upper arm muscles) he is not able to press down. For example, he can lift up the arm of his wheelchair, but he is unable to press a button. In order to do both one must have the complete set of muscles. If there is a need for him to press downward, he has learned to rotate his shoulder muscles by turning his hand downward and uses the strength from his shoulder muscles only. This ability allows him to drive.

When Rick was initially injured he was completely paralyzed from the nipple line down. The only thing he could move was his head. By the time he completed three months in the rehab hospital, he was able to move his neck muscles, shoulders, both elbows and his right wrist slightly. This amount of movement allowed him to feed himself with a splint and a bent utensil. He was unable to dress himself, comb his hair or shave, and of course, he had to be lifted into and out of bed.

While he was in the rehab hospital, I consulted an old timer who had cared for hundreds of quadriplegics. Apparently it sometimes takes ten years or more for quadriplegics to establish themselves in their new life.

When Rick came home from rehab, he had the expected spasms. These were a reflex due to the injury and sometimes were severe enough to almost cause him to slip out of his wheelchair. A member of our family was always with him. If he slipped down or tipped forward someone would prop him upright again. This happened many times a day and each of us went to Rick automatically to right him. As the years past this happened less frequently.

As time passed Rick learned to make use of every movement remaining in his body. It was a learning process that occurred automatically. With the remaining biceps, though not the triceps, he slowly became able to accomplish many tasks. Because he could pull up but not push down, he learned to type on his computer by dropping his little left bent finger on each key. In other words he learned to take advantage of gravity. It was because he was able to innovate in so many ways that made it possible for him to drive a modified vehicle.

Initially he was unable to turn pages of a book. He soon learned to use his little fingernail to turn the pages. It is amazing that after more than thirty years how many little things he is now able to do. He can hold an electric shaver with both palms of his hand and shave himself. While in the shower the nurse places a terry cloth mitt in his hand so that he can wash his own front.

When we have Rick with us for dinners and his favorite hors d'oeuvres are served, it takes him a few minutes to plan his mode of attack. Although his fingers are immovable, he sweeps the goodies into the palm of his hand and from there to his mouth. Rick constantly is striving for his independence. As the attendant had warned, it takes many years to develop these abilities. Each is a major triumph.

The day Rick earned his driver's license was a red-letter day. A whole new world was opened to him after being somewhat homebound for six years. His health had improved and had reached a plateau where all he needed was good care and diet.

Now to the van! We know, of course, that a vehicle's classy appearance is of utmost importance to any twenty-two-year-old. So after having a jazzy dune buggy and driving our sporty Mustang, Rick wanted his vehicle to look appropriately classy. This called for new mag wheel covers to replace the original drab ones; however, these led to future unfortunate occurrences. The van did not come carpeted so Tony and a carpet installer did the job. The van became a vision in gray with gray leather seats to match the carpeting. Rick was delighted, and we were happy for him.

The van had been modified to meet Rick's needs but there were some problems in the operation that Rick had to work out. The original conversion consisted of lowering the entire floor and raising the roof. A lift was installed on the side. He built a wireless remote to open and close the van doors and to raise and lower the lift. The steering wheel had to be raised as well and made smaller in diameter. Rick did not feel comfortable using the steering apparatus. "My hand constantly slipped off," he said. So, my innovative son designed a steering device, which utilized a single pin that could support the splint on his wrist. Clamps were installed on the floor to secure the wheelchair so that it could not move while driving. Rick also had to fasten himself in the wheelchair with a belt around his chest so his body would not tip forward when the brakes were applied. The upholstered standard driver's seat was removable so the average driver could place it under the steering wheel and use the van.

Rick had to use both hands to drive. The brake and gas handles were made to be very sensitive to the touch. He was able to put his left hand in a specially made grip to brake by an upward movement and to apply the gas with a downward push.

When the van was ready for Rick's use, he had to practice driving. It had been over six years since he had driven. At first, my husband took him to an empty parking lot, where he could reverse, turn corners and park; all maneuvers needed to pass the driver's test. After several lessons my husband had Rick drive home. He did so without a problem. He was now ready to take the driver's test at the Registry of Motor Vehicles. He passed the test, received his license and now was able to drive himself to college. It was not easy as a mother watching my son drive off for the first time. A prayer went up to the Lord asking Him to keep my son safe. As any mother, I was worried about his driving—so I did a lot of praying.

Driving meant Rick could do many errands for Lori and himself, including grocery shopping, dry cleaning and banking. Often he took off jauntily with his grocery list. Once in the store, a clerk walked with him through the aisles, while he made his selections. The clerk helped him thorough the checkout and placed the groceries in the van. When Rick arrived home, Lori unloaded. He was thrilled to be able to shop at the pet store where he could select tropical fish for his aquarium. He would arrive home proud of his plastic bag of water and the gorgeous fish.

Driving also made Rick's college attendance easier for Lori. Although he was now in his second year, he had several more years to go before his graduation.

One day Rick forgot to secure the wheelchair to the floor of the van. Fortunately he was driving slowly when the wheelchair rolled backwards. The van was in the drive position and moved forward causing a minor accident. He hit a stone wall causing the bumper to crush into the wheels. A tow truck had to be called. They were able to pull the bumper away from the wheels, so Rick could drive himself home. This was only the first incident—several more were to follow. It upset Rick to see the van damaged. He was not hurt and I hoped that this was a lesson he would never forget. He eventually established an accident-free record for several years.

However, one day Rick was traveling down a side road when he felt the van acting strangely. There certainly was something wrong. One of his front wheels had come completely off and the van tipped to one side. A kind woman, living in a nearby house, saw him, checked to see if he was hurt and then called my husband for help. Fortunately Tony was home, arrived with a tire jack and quickly replaced the wheel and the fancy wheel cover. The mag wheel covers most certainly caused this problem. When my husband had installed them, Rick had watched carefully to be sure the procedure was done correctly. He had instructed my husband not to tighten the nuts too much lest he would damage the new wheel covers—so there was no damage to the flashy wheel covers but only a tilted van in the street.

Each Christmas season Rick, Lori and Zoe traveled two hours to Worcester to celebrate the holiday with Lori's family and us. This particular van had a tendency to stall sometimes, and mechanics never seemed to be able to find the problem. This made me feel very uneasy.

It was Christmas Eve and Lori was driving. The day was one of the coldest of the year. The temperature was twenty below zero. They were about three miles from home when the van stalled. All electrical systems stopped functioning which meant no heater and no automatic wheelchair lift. Now the problem was, how to get Rick out. My husband was on duty at the fire station that evening and was called. The squad came to his rescue. Somehow the van was started and limped the rest of the way home. Fortunately, Rick was not alone. Lori, Zoe and I were with him. It was late in the evening and the extremely cold weather worried me. We had no blankets with us to wrap around Rick. The fire department responded quickly but the entire incident dampened our Christmas.

Another time when the van had been running well for a while, my husband received a call from Rick with the news that he was stuck in the vehicle. The cable that operated the lift had snapped. Tony immediately bought new cables and with Rick's help replaced the broken one. Once again luck was with us and my husband was available to help. This situation happened often enough that Rick kept extra cables in his garage. There seemed to be never a dull moment.

Another time, while driving the van, Rick felt something unusual. This time he was on the state highway traveling at a

good speed. Once again one of his front wheels came off causing the van to tip to one side. He calmly stopped the van and
a state trooper came to his rescue. The state trooper replaced
the wheel and Rick continued on his way. How was Rick so
lucky so often as to pull out of these situations—which could
have been extremely serious—without major difficulty? I
genuinely believe that the good Lord was watching over him
and had answered my prayers.

Eventually we had to face the fact that the van was getting
old with over one hundred thousand miles on it. It was now
five years old. It was time to consider purchasing a new one.
Rick began looking over brochures trying to decide what
vehicle would serve him best. As before, the van was selected
and then sent to a specialty modification factory to install
needed equipment. Three or four months were needed for the
modifications. The new van, a jazzy cranberry color, felt different to Rick. He had to become accustomed to the newness
of the vehicle but before long he was once again happily driving. This time there were no mag wheel covers and no difficult carpet installation. Eventually he felt this van was supe-
rior to the previous one. There was no more stalling.

Rick had been driving for several years without a mishap,
but that was about to end one day as he was on his way to
exercise Kali, his Rottweiler and his neighbor's dog, Indy, a
mongrel lab golden retriever combination, in an open area
near by. Both dogs were fully grown.

In May 1980, it was a clear day and Rick was traveling
about thirty miles an hour when he came over a slight rise in
the road and saw a Cadillac pull to a stop as it approached an
intersection from his right. Because the Cadillac had stopped,
Rick continued to drive through the intersection. Suddenly,

the driver of the Cadillac pulled out without looking in Rick's direction. Rick immediately slammed on his brakes, but the front of his van hit the driver's door of the other car. The Cadillac was knocked about seventy-five feet and the van came to rest against a telephone pole.

When the officers arrived on the scene, they could not get near Rick. The dogs were protecting him and would not let the police officers approach. A dog officer was called but to no avail. Finally Adria had to be summoned at her work to come and remove the dogs. Rick was taken to the hospital, as was the woman who drove the other car. Fortunately, neither of them needed treatment and both were released.

Rick's wheelchair was badly bent and the van was severely damaged. His wheelchair was taken to a welding shop to be repaired and Rick used an old one kept for such an emergency. The van took months to repair. In the meantime, Rick's life style was severely affected. He was unable to get to college or to run his errands. But, as usual, Rick found a way. The supermarket was approximately three miles from home. With his usual determination he covered the distance in his wheelchair and managed fairly well until the van was completely repaired. Soon Rick was traveling again in his van and was relieved that he did not have to replace it.

A few years later Rick was involved in another mishap. This time it was not so severe. While driving Rick must use both hands. One hand steers while the other hand works the brakes and gas. This makes it necessary to rely totally on mirrors when backing up. Late one rainy evening, when the windows were fogged and there were droplets of water on the mirrors, Rick backed out of the driveway and into a car which was parked directly across the street. There were neither streetlights nor lights on at the house, and the driveway was on an uphill slope. Rick was not moving fast, perhaps only three or four miles per hour. Nevertheless he damaged the other car and his own van. Once again no one was hurt, and there was some solace in the fact that on such a night the accident could have happened to anyone.

Not all of the "adventures" in the van were negative. For instance one Fourth of July weekend Rick piled all the neighborhood children and their parents into the van to go to Hyannis to see the fireworks. The kids were delighted but none of them were more delighted than Rick, who liked doing things for others. Another time, when an elderly woman in a wheelchair needed transportation to a doctor's appointment, Rick drove her. He takes such efforts for granted. It is second nature to him.

Recently the phone rang in Rick's office. It was his girl-friend, Julie. She had hit a curb and had a flat tire. Rick told her to call someone for service but she had no road service coverage. Rick felt he should go to her rescue. I was close by and at his request put a jack and special wrenches in his van. When I questioned Rick on how he could effectively change a flat tire, he said he could walk Julie through it and off he went.

I have an elderly brother in a nursing home who was to celebrate his eighty-fifth birthday at his grandson's home. Rick went to the nursing home, had my brother wheeled into the van and drove him to the party without difficulty. Another time he transported a woman who was a double amputee to her doctors appointment. He was happy to do it. He is able to focus on the positive and see how something good could come from his tragedy.

Today Rick has his fourth modified van. It is beautiful with all leather upholstery and a television in the rear for his passengers. When I first saw it, I was excited. When I asked Rick how he liked it he replied, "I hate it." I was taken aback. He was accustomed to the old van and its controls and had to get use to this new one. Not everyone likes change and this was an example of how the little things can make life more difficult for the handicapped than for the physically normal person. In this case, it didn't take long for Rick to master the new controls, and his initial distress was quickly forgotten.

CHAPTER TWELVE

INVENTIONS

Rick cannot exercise. He does not have enough useable muscles that he can work out. Without physical activities his body does not tire and therefore he is not a good sleeper. He cannot turn off his active mind and so he lies awake trying to solve problems. Lying awake at night is different for him. When we are restless at night tossing and turning we can get out of bed, raid the refrigerator, get a hot drink or read. Rick can only turn his head from side to side. A few times due to a lack of communication, the person who was to put him in bed did not arrive. He sat in his wheelchair all night with his head on his dining room table, until the morning nurse arrived. He had a cell phone on his wheelchair and was capable of making a call for help, but he has a hard time asking to have things done for him. He certainly did not want to disturb his parents at a late hour. Those nights were his worst nights.

Rick wanted to improve his life by making it easier for his caregivers and for himself. He believes there is a solution to every problem, and Rick is a natural problem solver. For example, he was always embarrassed to ask for help to empty his urinary leg bag. It was important to him to find a way to handle the job himself. When he started driving again, he had regained some independence, and he was looking for ways to be less dependent on others.

In 1981 while living in his Harwich apartment Rick started to do research to find a way to empty his urinary leg bag by himself. Eventually he invented a simple valve operated by a switch that allowed him to open and close the urinary leg bag on his own. What a relief. It also helped improve his health because it enabled him to increase his fluid intake and in turn reduce the frequency of urinary tract infections.

Rick spent many hours in the library researching reference books and listing companies he could contact for the specific items needed to assemble his equipment. He contacted more than thirty companies before he was able to find a valve suitable for his use. The valve had to be lightweight highly corrosion resistant and with an orifice of at least 15-21 hundredths of an inch, the larger the better. It also had to run on a 24-volt direct current. Because the valve would be worn on the leg, it could weigh no more than eight ounces. It had to be approximately three inches long and one inch in diameter including the hose connection on each end. The completed valve had many parts including coil housing, coil, washer and plunger, plastic fittings for the hoses, a switch, wiring for connecting it to the batteries on the wheelchair.

Rick experimented with three or four different types before he finally found the perfect small, stainless steel, non-corrosive valve. My husband assembled the valve under Rick's specific directions. The valve worked very well, and so Rick decided to put it on the market for others to enjoy the wonderful freedom it allowed. The size of the valve makes it easy to conceal under a pant leg for privacy. The switch used to operate the emptier can be located anywhere on the wheelchair, depending on individual needs and is operated simply by hitting a switch. There are also some special options available, which include a battery and charger for use with a manual wheelchair and a puff switch for individuals with severe mobility impairment.

Marketing his product became the second problem. Rick designed brochures and had them printed. But when the first brochures arrived he was not pleased with the colors. He wanted just the right tones. The printer soon realized this customer expected perfection. The brochures had to be corrected a few times to please Rick. Rick also produced booklets on his computer to give the user instructions, made prices lists, and ordered boxes and labels for shipping.

One day in 1983, Rick called me and proudly announced that he had started his own business: R. D. Equipment. He had given the business a name, and his next step was advertising, but he did not have money to do so. However, as usual, Rick came up with a grand idea to get around this problem. He wrote to several handicapped magazines and sent them his story. Most of them published articles about the valve under the category "Innovations." He also sent his story to a newspaper published by the Occupational Therapy Association. When they received his information they sent a reporter to his home. The reporter took pictures and published an excellent eye-catching article that appeared in the centerfold of the newspaper. Rick also had a large article titled "Survey of Manufactures of Incontinence Products" in the *Paraplegic News*

Magazine. There was an article published about his invention in *A Positive Approach Magazine*, a National Christian Magazine for the physically challenged person. Finally there was an article in *The Voice*, a newspaper published in Florida. Things were beginning to roll. The telephone rang off the hook with people looking to buy this new invention. Eventually he was able to formally advertise in many handicapped magazines.

My husband, now retired, was kept busy assembling the unit for sale. He set up a work area in the basement of our Cape home to do the work. Rick ordered the valves and my husband labeled each one with a special silver label. Then he put intake and output connectors on them for hoses and they were ready to be assembled. Harnesses were ordered with the switch and coil wire attached. Hose clamps were attached so the unit would fit over the chrome tubing of the wheelchair. The valve was attached to the harness and then tested. The boxes were ordered and shaped to fit the drain hose and completed valve along with the user's manual. Now they were ready to be shipped.

Rick had been using the Electric Leg Bag Emptier, as he named it, for several years, when there was an unfortunate occurrence. The switch that turned the emptier on and off had to be turned off manually after the bag was emptied. One day Rick forgot to turn the switch off. It became very hot and burnt an area on his ankle where the valve was touching his skin. Paralyzed people cannot feel such dangers as burns or frostbite. I was seriously concerned. The burn area was deep and healed only after months of treatment. This led Rick to send out a "product recall" to all his customers. Many customers returned the valve to have the switch replaced with a new one that turned itself off automatically.

The orders came in via telephone so Rick was often able to take some of the information with a pencil that he manipulated with his mouth. Most of the time he merely wrote the telephone number and tape-recorded the rest of the information. When I came in, I retrieved the information. Rick did the printing of the invoices on his computer, and my husband boxed and shipped the product. It was truly a family business. Some of the valves were shipped all over the world to such places as Guam, Switzerland, Scotland, Israel, the Philippines, Great Britain, Canada and all the states. Some of the customers wrote him to give their comments such as:

"I can't tell you how using the system has greatly increased my independence and mobility option," from Portland, Oregon.

"Your product has been selected because it has features we believe are important to show how assertive technology products make life easier for persons with disabilities," from a Rehabilitation Engineer, Virginia.

"Last spring I purchased your Electric Leg Bag Emptier. I am healthier because I no longer have to restrict fluid. Also, I am completely independent of having to ask for embarrassing assistance," from Melbourne, Florida.

"The original unit has performed flawlessly. I can't imagine doing without it," from Madison, New Jersey.

One can only imagine how proud the inventor was to receive such complimentary comments. What an enormous satisfaction, it gave Rick the incentive to create further products.

✤　　✤　　✤

Another challenge Rick faced was being able to bathe when he traveled. There was simply no way for him to get into a tub/shower. To solve this problem, Rick developed a shower he could use in any hotel room. It was made out of PVC pipe (white plastic tubing) and had a water proof liner with aluminum telescopic rods. It measured four feet by five feet with a shower curtain inside. A twenty-foot hose could be connected to the faucet of the bathroom sink to provide the shower water and an electric pump returned the waste water to the sink.

The shower was set up by his nurse much in a similar fashion to setting up a tent for camping. The entire portable shower could be folded and put into a suitcase the size of a golf bag. Rick used it twice without a problem, once visiting in Colorado and again at Disney World in Florida. The device had a built-in ground fault circuit for safety, but Rick was aware that he could not market it because of the electricity and water combination.

After some thought, he decided to design a chair in which he could slide above the side of a tub and under the shower head. The idea was to create an apparatus that did not need electricity and that could be used without altering the existing bathroom. And, of course, the device had to be designed so that it would not tip as his weight was transferred from one side of the tub to the other.

Rick made the initial sketch of his shower chair on the computer. He brought the illustration to a young fellow in New Bedford, Massachusetts, who was a stainless steel welder. The young welder manufactured the original chair in his garage. Rick traveled to New Bedford several times to work with him until the chair was completed. This was his first prototype.

Rick was planning a trip to Hawaii and had the chair shipped to the hotel. This new invention made a great impression on the Hawaiian nurse caring for Rick. It worked beautifully. The nurse was so impressed with the invention that she wrote to Rick to tell him so and recommended the chair to other handicapped people. Her testimonial is sent to anyone inquiring about the tub slide shower chair.

Obviously traveling is far from easy for the handicapped. Rick spends many hours making plans for his accommodations, not only for the flight and room but also for a wheelchair accessible van to be available at his destination. Most of the time, he uses his computer to book what he needs.

When Rick arrived home, he had plenty of work ahead of him. He made blueprints of his shower chair and contacted several manufacturing companies in the hope that one would produce the chair. He found a manufacturer in Worcester, which made for easy communication.

Rick thought it would be a great idea for hotels to buy the chair for their handicapped guests. He mailed hundreds of letters around the country, but to his disappointment only a few hotels were interested. He next approached the medical profession, through rehabilitation centers, nursing homes and hospitals. Here the response was much more enthusiastic. The telephone again began to ring.

Diana, Rick's girlfriend at this time, had traveled with him to Hawaii and knew exactly how the chair worked. Diana was a divorcée without children, the same age as Rick. She was a brunette with a petite build, and she worked in her father's restaurant in Falmouth. Of course, Diana was an excellent cook. She moved in with Rick and served meals that had a gourmet flare.

Diana had many fine talents and traits along with her good looks. She was an excellent worker and accomplished more in a day than the average person would in a week, but she had bouts of depression. She often spoke to me about this problem. She was one of four girls from a loving family, but somehow depression would make its unhappy appearance without warning. She attributed it to her genes. Her grandmother too was a depressed person. Rick tried hard to elevate her spirits but nothing seemed to help.

Diana and Rick put their business heads together and put the tub slide shower chair on the market. Plans were made to participate in a trade show in New York City at the Jacob Javits Convention Center. Fortunately for Rick, his nurse, Denny, was able to go with them. The show was a big success, and it marked the beginning of a lot more work for Rick as he promoted his business.

In 1995, about one year after he invented the chair, the sales began. Rick employed Diana to work in his office as a sales representative, a job she held for many years. She also traveled to trade shows in many parts of the United States to demonstrate the new equipment. When Diana was away, I helped in the office taking orders, filing, sending statements and writing checks. Rick is capable of answering the telephone, taking telephone numbers with a pencil in his mouth, writing a few letters, and putting a piece of paper in the printer—he has developed a technique that is too complicated to explain.

Unfortunately, for reasons unbeknownst to me their relationship began to fade. Diana moved out and rented an apartment in Hyannis about five miles away but continued to work in Rick's office. For a year their relationship was clumsy and uncomfortable. It was all business and nothing else. Tony and I were saddened to see this happen. We admired Diana. She was sincere and a good worker but they both agreed the separation was for the best.

The orders for the "Tub Slide Shower Chair" as it was named, come in from all over the United States and Canada.

A primary reason for its sales success is that it is easy to use. The armrests swing away from the seat to permit entry and exit from the seat. The leg members of the outrigger are adjustable to alter the height of the outrigger. The outrigger slides on a track. The chair has four wheels to move it from bedroom to bathroom and then over the standard bathtub. The Tub Slide Shower Chair is unsurpassed in safety and simplicity, as it allows a disabled individual the same comfort and convenience which was previously available only from a roll-in-shower. It is an inexpensive alternative to major bathroom renovations, and makes any bathroom accessible. It is convenient for travel and there is no difficulty using the chair abroad. It is easy to assemble, to clean, to dismantle and store. What makes the TSSC unique is the outrigger that attaches to the side. This allows the top of the shower chair, including the seat, arms and back to slide over a bathtub. Having everything move as a unit makes the patient comfortable, stable and secure.

The chair can also roll over a standard toilet. Thus a person can use the toilet without having to be moved from the chair and the person can use a standard bathroom with minimal assistance. That is a benefit to both physical and mental health. Who wants an audience when using the facilities?

In May of 1996 Rick finally received a U.S. Patent for the Tub Slide Shower Chair.

To promote this item, Rick had another idea. He decided to take a mini course at the Cape Cod Local Channel on making a video. Here he produced a six-minute video illustrating how to use the TSSC. It featured well-qualified people to promote the product such as Dr. Michael Ackland, an orthopedic surgeon, Denny, Rick's nurse who is a rehabilitation specialist, Diana, his sales representative and Rick with his big-as-life smile. He sent hundreds of these videos to inquiring customers all over the United States, Canada and Hawaii.

These innovations have kept Rick busy. He could be even more creative, if time would only permit. He has been using a folding fork for several years. It is an item Rick made for himself and finds handy at home as well as in a restaurant. It is a stainless steel fork that has a hinge much like the hinge on a jackknife. It opens and closes easily and is easily carried on his wheelchair. He now has several hundred of these ready for sale. This time the item will be listed in a catalog and he will not be handling it himself as he did before. With Rick's quick mind these will undoubtedly not be his final creations. One never knows what he will come up with next.

There was once a time when there was a lull in the activities in his office. We sat, chatted, and Rick musingly remarked, "Mom, did you ever think I would be doing this?" He knew he had never been a good student and had completely frustrated Tony and me with his lack of interest in school. In this creative area he has found his niche.

Rick works very hard tending to his business but obviously finds time to enjoy life as much as possible. Each winter for the past several years, he relaxes on vacation in a warm climate. It takes hours of planning to have a nurse, his girlfriend, and his medical equipment on hand for him, as well as a wheelchair accessible vehicle, but he is always determined. He has traveled to Mexico, the Caribbean, Florida, Puerto Rico, the Dominican Republic and Hawaii. It seems nothing stops him. He just goes and goes. It is unfortunate he is handicapped with his horrible physical problems and yet fortunate to be able to do all these nice things. To be able to be positive is important to Rick and our family.

CHAPTER THIRTEEN

NEW HOME

Eighteen years after Rick's accident. Adria, his most recent girlfriend, had moved on. Rick wasn't lonely. The family who lived upstairs took Rick under their wing, fed him and helped him with many of his needs. Denny, his nurse, came for four hours each morning. Then Rick spent from three in the afternoon until nine at night at the college. Later in the evening, Donna came to put him to bed. So his days were filled with activities.

Rick had lived comfortably in his apartment for fifteen years. The neighborhood friends treated Rick with kindness and were always wonderfully helpful. But he wanted a change. His business was growing fast enough to allow him to save money. He bought a house lot and sold it a year later for a sizeable profit.

Rick spent a lot of his free time with Mike, a building contractor. Rick was very interested in acquiring real estate and he and Mike discussed the pros and cons of buying a lot.

Mike lived in West Barnstable. He invited Rick to see the house he had built for himself. Rick took to the area immediately. There were many pluses for him. It was closer to the college and to Worcester, making a trip to the Cape shorter. So he and Mike cruised the area scouting for lots for sale. In West Barnstable they found some very attractive lots that had an adjoining swimming pool and tennis court. These were great assets for the affluent, but they seemed to be out of Rick's price range.

A few days later, Rick met a real estate appraiser at the college. Naturally they discussed real estate and it turned out that the properties that Rick was interested in were to be auctioned. They were part of a subdivision that had been planned but never built. The builder had run into financial problems and a bank foreclosed on the property. A day after their meeting, the real estate appraiser brought Rick a flyer advertising the auction.

Rick decided to go to the auction. When he arrived, there were fifteen other people interested in the properties. Two lots were on the auction block. One of them seemed perfect for Rick. It was on the straight part of the road. Rick wanted to bid for it. He was ready to make a purchase with a five thousand dollar check in hand for a down payment, but the bidding started at thirty-five thousand dollars, well beyond what Rick was prepared to spend, and the lot was sold to someone else.

The second lot was on the curve of the road. The back of the property was next to a swimming pool and tennis court. It really did not appeal to Rick. He was discouraged to the point of not even wanting to bid on it. When the bidding started on the second lot, Rick made a low bid of twenty-five thousand dollars. No one else was interested and Rick made it clear that he would not go higher. So instead of out-bidding Rick the bank officers let Rick get it at his price.

Of course, parents are kept in the dark and are the last to know. I lead an active life and usually when I am in Worcester I am not home in the middle of the afternoon. However, on this afternoon I was home when the phone rang. It was my son calling to tell me he had just bought a house lot. I could tell by his voice that he was wildly excited. He bought the lot to build his own home. He had lived in that lower level apartment for fifteen years and it was time for a change.

I was excited for him but also somewhat concerned. How would he manage all this? I told myself that Rick was extremely capable and would do just fine. Ten days after the auction he paid for the lot in full. When he received the deed, his lawyer told him about a technicality. He would have to wait for 120 days or four months before he could build, in case the former owner decided to buy the lot back. During this period, to avoid thinking of that awful possibility, Rick drew assorted floor plans on his computer. He knew exactly what he wanted. Thank goodness, Mike was with him to give him much needed help.

In his spare time Rick drove to the lot and sat in his van, analyzing and dreaming about his future home and planning a way to place the house to its best advantage. He wanted privacy. He was concerned about the swimming pool and tennis court in the rear of the lot, and the fact that the lot was on the curve of the road. All these things called for serious thought. The 120 days had not passed, but Rick and the builder were anxious to get started. It was August. It was a momentous day in 1990, a few days after the devastating Hurricane Bob had hit the Cape, when they started to clear the lot. Rick had just celebrated his thirty-fifth birthday. What a great way to celebrate.

When Rick and Adria were still together, they had visited a friend who had a beautiful post and beam home. Rick was crazy about it and dreamed of having one that was similar. He busied himself on his computer and eventually drew plans and more plans. He spent hours trying to get the best arrangement for his personal needs. He eventually developed the perfect home.

The lot had a good size frontage, but Rick was more interested in his backyard. It was to become the most important part of his plan. There was no trouble excavating for the basement. But it was a different story once the hole was dug. The torrential rains filled the hole and Rick had an unwanted swimming pool. Electric pumps had to be hired to drain the water out so that building could take place. Fortunately, this was the only problem that occurred during the entire time the house was being built. Rick savored every minute of the construction.

The plans Rick had drawn on his computer naturally specified post and beam construction. The frame came from a company in Vermont and in one day the exterior of his house was up. It was an amazing thing to watch. With a specially equipped truck, the beams were put into place. Rick was like an eager little kid watching the progress at the site every day. The builders worked all winter using heaters to supply heat inside the house. The house was completed in April 1991.

The house has an office, living room, dining area, two baths and two bedrooms, one of which is in the loft. The exterior construction has simple lines with an attached two-car garage. Above the garage is a studio apartment for part of his staff. The entire exterior of the house has a rustic motif. The house is stained brown without shutters, and in place of a lawn there are wood chips.

The front door opens into a living room and dining room area about thirty by twenty feet. The floors are hardwood, the walls white with cathedral ceilings. The beams are stained and the ceiling has seven recessed lights. There are two skylights in the rear. The fireplace is made of red brick and extends up to the cathedral ceiling. It boasts a raised hearth. Hung on the center of the brick fireplace is a huge grapevine wreath, made by Adria. The mantel is made from one enormous stained beam and is held in place by three red bricks that are placed in tier fashion. This beautiful fireplace is the focal point of Rick's living area.

There are six windows in the front of the house. A large antique spinning wheel decorates the two windows on one side of the living room. A red plaid camel back sofa sits at a right angle to the fireplace with matching throw pillows. On the opposite side of the room sits a green club chair and an old fashion rocker. My husband made a solid oak butler's table that is used between these chairs. Underneath the butler's table is an oriental rug. Except for this rug all the floors are left free of carpeting because of the wheelchair. Next to the fireplace is a beautiful oak entertainment center designed by Rick and built by Tony and Rick's cousin, James Pickett. At a right angle to the entertainment center is a French door, which leads to the deck and eventually to the backyard.

The kitchen is built to accommodate a wheelchair. The surface unit of the stove has space underneath so the wheelchair can fit if Rick needs to get to the unit. The same design was used under the sink with a window above it that looks out into the backyard. The oak kitchen cabinets are custom made, and the microwave and wall oven are built into the cabinets. He selected a black and white checkerboard pattern tile for the counter tops and a bright red tile floor, a striking feature to the room.

In Rick's office there is a four-foot deep dark green formica counter that takes up one entire wall. It is here that he keeps his fax machine, credit card machine and telephone along with several files. Once again the entire underside of the counter is left open for his wheelchair. His computer, printer, copying machine and file cabinet are located on the opposite side of the room. Rick designed the computer desk with a recessed lower shelf so that his knees do not hit it while he works on the computer.

A guest bathroom is located opposite his office. It is a standard size bathroom with standard fixtures. The red tiled kitchen floor extends into this bathroom and the walls are tiled in black and white.

Rick's bedroom has a queen-size waterbed moved from his former basement apartment. The two night tables have conventional storage for his medical supplies. There is direct access from the bed to the bathroom roll-in-shower. A door from the bathroom leads to the deck that has an outdoor shower, which Rick uses in the summer. Both showers have thermostatic control mixing valves. All the doors in the house have openings that are thirty inches wide to permit easy passage of Rick's wheelchair. Most of the doors are sliding doors, which makes it easy for Rick to slip his hand in the handle and open them. Although the design and planning lends itself to wheelchair accessibility, the house does not look like a health facility. Actually all new homes should be built with some of these handicap features.

The swimming pool at the rear of the lot had been abandoned and had become a paradise for frogs and toads. Rick had it drained and Tony scrubbed the interior. Before long it was useable.

An electric garage door opener operates the garage door. The kitchen door opens with an automatic opener. It has a large round disc that one pushes and the door automatically opens. Rick enters the basement by way of a freight elevator on a moving platform. It resembles a forklift only without the truck. There are no doorknobs in the house. All doors have a pull down latch. Instead of regular switches, the light switches are push levers. The bathroom mirror over the sink was lowered. All these minor adjustments make Rick's home very comfortable.

All the window treatments are done in the same style, a simple swag. I went to the fabric store to bring Rick samples, and he picked out his colors. I made the shower curtains and window treatments for the entire house. It was certainly a labor of love.

This house is just right for Rick—small with a Colonial façade and a marvelous backyard that looks typical Cape Cod with lots of pine trees. Many family members visit and use the outdoor swimming pool. To Rick, this house is his sanctuary. It's peaceful. When it is rainy and cold, he has his fireplace lit and when it is summer all the windows are wide open. The wonderful breezes of Cape Cod and the Atlantic Ocean stream in. He loves it. We love it.

✤ ✢ ✤

After spending twelve years in his beautiful post and beam home, Rick felt he needed to do some renovating. The deck in the rear of the house looked fine to me, but he wanted it removed and replaced with a larger one. He and his friend, Jim Nally, a deck builder, spent many hours planning the new mahogany deck. It was designed with two benches at one end with a canopy over it so one can relax with a drink and view the fishpond. The plan was to have a hot tub on one side of the deck; Rick searched and searched to find one to his liking. He selected a hot tub large enough for five people. There were two seats on one side and a bench on the opposite side. The hot tub was set to be eighteen inches above the deck making it easy to get into. Rick used his computer to design a "boom." He took the drawing to a welding shop to have the boom made. The boom was painted black and was anchored in three feet of cement. Bearings were used so that it could turn 360 degrees. An electric hoist was purchased and mounted on top of the boom.

When most of the work was completed, there was still the problem of how to get Rick into the water. He had a Hoyer lift but it proved to be impractical. It meant that Rick would have to be removed from his wheelchair and placed on his bed. The sling of the Hoyer lift would have to be put under him, and he would be placed back in the chair and then hook himself onto the hoist.

Rick found a more practical apparatus called a Handi Move. Metal pieces with adjustable straps are placed under each thigh and a corset-like clamp covered with black leather hugs his upper torso. With the use of the electric switch, Rick is raised out of his wheelchair and into the hot tub. He enjoys this new activity, the result of days of planning.

There were more improvements planned. Rick wanted more living space in his home, and it was at this time that he decided to renovate the basement into an office and a recreation room. The elevator was the only means of getting into the basement. He wanted a staircase built which required an addition to the house. His plan had to be approved by the town's building inspectors. But when the blue prints were submitted they were not approved. Apparently the turn of the stairs did not meet the building code.

Rick spent many hours on his computer printing a new set of plans, which were finally approved. The basement was partitioned so half was an unfinished storage area. The finished area had terra cotta tiles on the floor and soft light green walls and was furnished with brown leather furniture and a huge new television set. It is a quiet place where one can escape from the upstairs activities of phone calls and visitors.

There will probably be more projects in the future. It is Rick's nature to come up with new ideas, and it is a way to keep his mind occupied and not focused on his injury.

CHAPTER FOURTEEN

RELATIONSHIPS

In the nineties when Rick worked in the college computer lab, he met several attractive women students among them was a nursing student named Regina. He showed Regina how to produce her term paper on the computer, which helped her achieve a high grade. She and Rick soon became good friends. Rick attended her graduation ceremonies and continued to date Regina. He courted her in his usual manner with invitations to dinners, movies and small gifts. She eventually took a position as a staff nurse in a Colorado hospital, and before long she invited Rick to visit her. Without hesitation he packed his belongings and went off to Colorado. During the visit Rick and Regina had some serious conversations about the future. Rick was still not ready to settle down. Rick returned home and the relationship ended.

In no time at all Rick met another appealing woman, Diana, while she was preparing her homework in the lab. As we saw in the last chapter, Diana became an important part of Rick's life both in business and as a companion. And even after their relationship ended Diana continued to be very important to Rick's business.

On Christmas day 1998, Diana was returning to her apartment in Hyannis from her parents' home in Falmouth when her Volkswagen Jetta hit a patch of ice and slid off the road into a ditch. Rick received a scary call from her parents saying she had been airlifted to a Boston Hospital with severe internal injuries. She was hospitalized for several weeks, but thankfully she eventually returned to work. She continued to work as Rick's sales representative for many years. .

After Diana moved out, Rick decided that he did not want another woman to live with him. He wanted to live alone. I didn't like that idea. It seemed to me that he needed help for various simple tasks. It had been over twenty years since his injury. Even though he learned to do many tasks such as taking a plate out of the microwave oven, making telephone calls, and writing with a pencil in his mouth, I was not convinced the solitary life was for him. For instance there is one problem he had been unable and is still unable to solve. Much to his extreme frustration when he drops something he cannot retrieve it. There are gadgets on the market today for this problem but his fingers are too paralyzed for him to use any of them. When he built his home, he made provisions for someone to live in the studio apartment over his garage. He hired a succession of nursing students from the college, who lived above the garage, to put him to bed at night and care for him during the day. For a long time, this arrangement worked well.

In 1997, Rick met Julie, a student at the college, who was working part-time in the counseling office while taking some courses. She was divorced and had a five-year-old daughter,

Jessica. She also spent time in the computer lab doing her homework. Rick became Jessica's baby sitter. Rick handled the job with ease and enjoyed entertaining the little girl while her mother worked on her papers. This arrangement went on for about a year. Rick and Julie were just friends, nothing more.

One evening Rick was out with some friends socializing in a small restaurant. Julie was with some of her girl friends celebrating her first permanent job since motherhood. She was seated directly across from Rick and in his eyes she was the most gorgeous women he had ever seen. She was breathtakingly radiant. He definitely wanted to date her. She was trying to recover from a bad marriage and the loss of her grandmother whom she had loved dearly. Julie was in no mood to date anyone. They met a few times at different college functions. Before long Rick was sending her flowers and pleading for a date. Eventually he won her over.

And so Julie, her daughter and Rick began enjoying each other's company. They vacationed together, saw one another over the weekends and attended Jessica's school activities.

During the years Julie and Rick dated, she spent weekends in his home. Rick would often buy very special foods to have dinner for two by candlelight while Jessica spent weekends with her father. Rick was always excited and looked forward to an intimate dinner for two. How romantic! While I worked in his office, I would help with some of the preparations for these special dinners. He loved every minute of this preparation and anticipation of having his date for the weekend.

This arrangement went on for a few years. Julie was living in Yarmouth and Jessica was enrolled at the Cape Cod Academy, a private school in Centerville. Julie worked in

Centerville with an engineering company as their secretary; this meant lots of traveling to chauffeur her daughter to school and activities. Later Rick and Julie agreed it would be easier for all of them to live under one roof. So Julie gave up her apartment and moved in with Rick. Jessica lives in the studio apartment over the garage. This arrangement has been working well. Jess calls Rick, her "Buddy." They appear happy which makes me happy too.

❦   ❦   ❦

Lori was among several of Rick's girlfriends who became a registered nurse. She bought a home in Harwich and is on the staff of the Visiting Nurses Association. Her daughter, Zoe was a very brilliant child, attended Trinity School in Harwich, and received a scholarship to Clark University in Worcester. After graduation she furthered her education at Brown University in Rhode Island. Zoe is married, living in the Boston area and has recently given birth to twin boys.

Adria became a registered nurse also. She moved to Arizona where she worked on an Indian Reservation. She married and had a son. When her son was a toddler she divorced and came east and settled in Randolph close to her family. She has attended Rick's Pig Roasts each year and proudly introduces her son Owen to all of us. When I last spoke to her she was working with the Public Health Department.

Diana remained with Rick, working in his office. She gave up her apartment and bought a beautiful four-bedroom home with an Olympic-size swimming pool in Hyannis. She lives there alone and enjoys working in her garden, planting exotic flowers and entertaining. She does not have a male friend. She told me that she could never find anyone who was as good to her as Rick.

Regina, the woman who Rick had a brief relationship with, I believe is still in Colorado. Rick and our family have lost track of her.

All the women who lived with Rick helped him and were helped by him. Most did not know what they wanted in life. They had no goals, college education or professions, but each went to college and graduated, as well as Julie who graduated after several years of attending night classes while she worked full time. It is very satisfying to see how successful each of them has become. These women have to be admired.

CHAPTER FIFTEEN

THE ACTIVE LIFE

The job insecurity that has settled over the nation during the past few years has made the idea of self-employment more appealing to college students. A number of colleges and universities are offering courses and even degree programs in entrepreneurship to prepare young people for the challenge of working for themselves. Would-be entrepreneurs realize they would rather work for themselves than someone else. They want the option of creating their own destiny. The college professors impress on the students that it's better to have tried and failed than not have tried at all. Self-employment means taking a lot of risks. Success in life and a career comes from proper planning. First comes a sound business plan. Then consideration must be given to such issues as competition and accounts receivable, advertising and marketing. But above all, customer service is paramount. Customers must be approached with enthusiasm, integrity and honesty.

Today, Cape Cod Community College offers courses for entrepreneurs. Unfortunately the courses were not available when Rick attended the college in the eighties. Rick's entre-preneurship was helped through his associations at the college while he was working in the computer lab. Several of the pro-fessors became involved with Rick's life and activities. Rick had no formal education in engineering when he started his business nor did he take any engineering courses. His ideas came from his instinctive understanding of engineering and much determination and hard work. Talent is never enough. He eventually received an associate's degree in liberal arts. He was even asked by the administration of the college to teach a course in entrepreneurship, but his credentials were not sufficient to accept the position.

One cold wintry day, while Rick and his friend Chuck Brewster, an insurance executive, were out to dinner, they discovered that they both felt depressed. Both were now doing well, but they each felt that something was missing even though they both led very full lives. Chuck was a single parent with two daughters. And, of course, Rick had his own challenges. But each felt a void, and in order to fill it they hit on a plan to form a charitable scholarship fund to help bud-ding entrepreneurs. They each donated one thousand dollars to start a bank account with the name on the account "Young Entrepreneurs of Cape Cod and the Islands," a nonprofit cor-poration. It was opened in February 2000. The goal was to create grants for graduating high school students to pursue entrepreneurship goals. The grant would be five hundred dollars to two high school students, a boy and a girl, each year.

Interested seniors in high school can apply for the grants. They are chosen on the basis of their interest and enthusiasm for the business world.

The girl who received the first grant wanted to design clothing. She stated in her letter of application that she enjoyed thrift shopping in Salvation Army and Goodwill stores where she searched for attractive fabrics to turn into dresses. She proudly wore outfits made from clothing she bought at thrift stores.

The boy who received the first grant also had a dream. From an early age, he wanted to fly, and he read everything he could find about aviation. He took his first flight lesson when he was twelve. By the time he was sixteen he had soloed. His long-term goal was to own a charter company.

After the first two students were selected, an attractive flyer was made to promote the organization. The local radio station had a question and answer program about the organization during which Rick and Chuck clearly stated their purpose and goals. To date they have given six grants to students with a dream. Best of all there are no administrator's expense; all monies that come in also go out.

�֍   ֍   ֍

The association Rick has with the college has always been amiable. They respect his natural business acumen, his engineering skills and problem solving ability. There are times when the computer that controls their electrical heating system goes awry. Rick is called in and with little difficulty solves their problem.

A section of the college between the North and South buildings had empty space. It was a waste of a valuable section of the college campus. The administrators decided to make the area a spot where the students could congregate at tables and chairs, have a soft drink and socialize. Rick met with the administrators and although he was busy with his own business, he took time to design the tables and chairs according to the administrators guidelines. He contacted a welding company and the chairs were designed with a base shaped like a "Z" and seats that swiveled. The art department selected the fabric and he had the chairs upholstered. The small round tables had a metal pedestal base and both tables and chairs were painted with a special black paint. The table tops were beautiful gray granite that was imported from Brazil. Months later the project was finally completed. All five tables and eight chairs were secured firmly to the concrete floor. It was a job well done according to the college personnel who were extremely pleased.

❦   ❦   ❦

Michael Bejtlich is Management Program Coordinator at Cape Cod Community College. One of his techniques to help students understand what is needed to establish a business is to have successful entrepreneurs speak to his classes. Each term he calls upon my son to be a guest speaker. Rick explains how he started his business and discusses finances and creating an objective business plan. He tells the students that it is important to know who are the competitors and who are the customers. And he stresses that the customer must come first, and that they must be approached with enthusiasm, integrity, honesty and determination.

After the college completed the North and South building connector, Michael planned a dedication ceremony to thank everyone who donated money and the students who worked to complete it. Rick was invited to attend the dedication but was unable to go because he was away on business. He suggested that I should take his place. I got myself all dressed up in my Sunday finery and attended. People there made me feel like a celebrity and praised my son for the work he had done on the furniture in the students lounge. At the same time, they gave awards to three students who produced the best business plans. One former student gave a talk on her accomplishments in starting a successful gift shop business and how she implemented her plan. The afternoon ended with delicious refreshments and music.

✼   ✼   ✼

Like anything else, when a wheelchair gets old, it has to be replaced. Spending over thirty years in a wheelchair has made my son fully aware of his needs. When it was time to order a new one, Rick searched for months to find one that he would like and would also be able to modify for his particular needs. He requested the manufacturer to leave it unpainted. When the wheelchair finally arrived it was too high and too wide. It could not fit under the steering wheel of his van and his knees could not fit under his dining table. Work had to be done on it and he knew even before the purchase the problems he would have rebuilding it. This was the start of months of adjusting and modifying the chair.

Rick used a computer program to plan the modification of his new wheelchair. Then he contacted an engineer at the University of Massachusetts Dartmouth, to work with him. The university has a program for engineering students to do work for local businesses. The students get experience and charge a minimal fee. Rick teamed up with Chen Lee, a design consultant, who had come to the United States from China to get a graduate degree. He and Rick worked together for months. Rick would give Chen suggestions and Chen would do all the calculations. It was a trying time for Rick because he had to travel 90 minutes twice a week to get to the campus and while he was driving he was unable to change his position to relieve pressure on his spine. But he loved the motivating and stimulating environment he found there.

Once the chair was designed, Rick contacted Bob Harrington, a machinist in the Mechanical Engineering Department at the University, to make the modifications. But first the chair had to be painted, and it had to be disassembled before bringing it to the paint shop. My husband took it apart with Rick's help. Once the painting was completed, the chair had to be reassembled. Adding the paint to the parts made the pieces difficult to fit into place. This frustrated Tony as well as Rick. After spending two days working on it, Rick finally called upon Bob, the machinist for assistance. All three men worked together and finally finished the job.

In a life such as ours there are days of anguish but also days of great joy. One morning, I was working in my son's office when he entered in a jaunty fashion in his new wheelchair. He appeared before me and suddenly he had risen to my height. "Mom, this is the first time in thirty years I have been able to talk with another person face to face." He could see the room and everything in it that was at this height. The visual expression on my son's face as he saw the world from an adult height was worth all the effort and months of frustration it took to get him there.

If only I had a camera to take a picture of his facial expression. He could now see the top of a shelf instead of just the bottom. It was like a blind person seeing for the first time. The joy we both experienced was immeasurable. Now that he can raise himself to an adult height, he usually raises himself when he greets people so they do not have to stoop to his level.

❦　❦　❦

Rick's creative ability flourishes with sparkling imagination in his personal life as well. His friend, Chuck Brewster, who lives in an elegant home in nearby Osterville, decided to have a Halloween party. Of course he approached Rick to produce the invitations from his computer as he had previously done for my college graduation celebration. This was to be a big party with many guests. There was to be a prize for the best, strangest, and sexiest costume. Naturally this unlocked Rick's competitive spirit. His first idea was to decorate his wheelchair as one would decorate a float for a parade and then to find a role for Julie, his girlfriend. What could be more challenging than a magician (Julie) popping a rabbit (Rick) out of a hat? Tony made a huge hat using a hoola hoop as the brim. The sides were cardboard and covered with black material. The hat was placed over the wheelchair. Rick bought a white sweat suit and wore it inside out making it appear fuzzy. He used pink chalk to make a pink belly. He wore socks turned inside out on his hands and colored the palms pink, sprayed his hair white, painted his face white, applied rouge to his cheeks and glued on whiskers. The pink ears where attached to his head to complete the rabbit.

The second part of the costume was the sexy part. Julie was dressed in a black lace camisole, with black stockings and high heel shoes. They rented a tuxedo with a long jacket and top hat. A bright colored piece of fabric was cut into the size of a handkerchief and stuck inside the sleeves as part of the magician act. A wand completed the costume, and then the nutty twosome was ready to go. Rick's wheelchair is one that rises and lowers therefore he was able to raise himself out of the hat. They won first prize, one hundred dollars worth of scratch tickets.

Naturally, the following year was another Halloween Party at Chuck's house. Rick had to put on his thinking cap to produce another crazy costume. This was going to be tough. How was he to compete with last year's huge success? Julie, of course, had to be included in his plan. He started six weeks before the party to make Aladdin and a genie on a magic carpet. Denny, his nurse was driving in to care for Rick one day and noticed an Old Persian rug at the roadside ready to be picked up for trash. It was perfect. She told Rick about it, he grabbed it, and proceeded to work with it for the next costume. He cut a three by five piece of rug as part of the costume. It was placed on a piece of plywood with a hole for Rick's body and then placed on his wheelchair. He stuffed legs of stretch pants and arranged them on top of the rug to produce the illusion of Aladdin in a sitting position. Costume jewelry was scattered on the carpet. Rick grew a beard for one month and dyed it black. He rolled a white bed sheet into a turban with gold braids for effect. Next was the sexy part. Julie custom tailored the genie costume she had bought to make it sexier, wore a black wig, put a gem in her belly button and lots of alluring makeup. This entire costume had to be assembled after they arrived at the party. Rick was not able to travel with the piece of plywood on his wheelchair. You guessed it again. They won first prize again.

✣   ✣   ✣

Rick's mind never seems to stop. He is now thinking of a new design to release urine from a leg bag. He has expressed his vision but has not begun work on it. I am excited about this new concept and am waiting to see the finished product.

His past inventions, the electric leg bag opener, the tub slide shower chair, the folding fork, the designing of the college lounge furniture and now a new invention is what makes Rick happy, busy and useful. His life is full. Success is a journey not a destination.

CHAPTER SIXTEEN

THE YEARLY BASH

Rick moved into his new home in August 1991. It was not long before he was planning a big party. He loves people and draws many to him. He is never lonesome. He sat at his computer in the office of his lovely post and beam home with his bent left little finger, hitting each key to produce the invitation to his annual pig roast. He meticulously planned every detail for a successful pig roast for his friends. Every year he prints 200 invitations. Each invitation gives specific details about this important day on the third Saturday of August. In the corner of each invitation is a picture of a pig and the statement "Your admission ticket is one unscratched lottery ticket. Pick a winner." If they wish, guests may bring their favorite dish or pastry. All drinks, meats, rolls, condiments, paper goods and utensils and the 100-pound pig are supplied by Rick. A four-piece band and a port-a-potty are also furnished.

If you know Rick, you are invited. He invites the friends he grew up with, his neighbors, his co-workers and even his stockbroker and his attorney. With all these people and his family, about 250 attend the bash.

The pig roast is held in his backyard, which has some unique features. The ground is covered with wood chips instead of grass to reduce maintenance. An interesting feature in his yard is a fishpond with channels of flowing water that create the pleasant sound of rippling water. The deck is where Rick can escape from his office each day to bask in the sun, view the pond, and hear the rippling water. It is a place for solitude and quiet reflection, a place he can shape his many dreams.

In preparation for the party, the entire pond is roped off so no one will lose their balance and fall into it. Attached to some of the trees are birdhouses and bird feeders that attract numerous interesting birds. The yard had a rustic appearance created by tall pines, birches and flower gardens where colorful annuals are planted. In the rear of the yard is a tennis court and Olympic-size swimming pool for the neighborhood families to use as part of the residential complex called "Weeks Crossing." There is a red brick fireplace in the center of the yard where huge pots of water are boiled and corn on the cob is cooked. One large barbeque grill is used to cook chicken, sausage, hamburgers and hot dogs. Tony puts on his apron, with the monogram printed: "Papa Tony, Grill Master" and does a wonderful job cooking all these meats to perfection.

The band sets up on the large wooden deck that adjoins Rick's living room. Ramps are connected to the deck that leads to the yard. Halfway around the house is a four-foot wide wooden walkway to accommodate Rick's wheelchair.

Two weeks before the party I help my son take an inventory of what needs to be purchased. "Do we have enough paper plates, cups and utensils?" Rick asks. I check everything. All supplies are stored neatly in boxes in his basement. He enters the elevator to get into the basement and points out the boxes that hold the party supplies. Rick knows where everything is kept.

Rick's entire family: my husband, son Bob, daughter Gina, his friends and I help set up for the occasion. Bob and my husband pick up the picnic tables and chairs. The tables are covered with white paper, and all the folding chairs are set around them. Rick does not feel it is necessary for everyone to have a chair because he has found that most people like to stand so they can move around and socialize. Lights are strung on all the trees and torches are lit the night of the party to deter insects. The 100-pound pig is ordered in advance and is picked up by Rick the day before the party. A wheelbarrow is cleaned and filled with ice and this is the pig's bed for the day.

On the day of the roast, Bob is in charge of roasting the pig. He has help tying the legs together and placing it on the spit. He is responsible for watching, turning, basting and tending to the pig on the rotisserie. For several years, Rick rented a barbeque grill large enough for this size roast. But one year the man who owned it refused to rent it. He said, "People are not taking care of it after they use it, and it's being returned in poor condition."

Rick faced a dilemma. He certainly wasn't ready to give up having the pig roast. He looked forward to the party each year. It was his way of showing his love for all his friends and of acknowledging his appreciation for all they do for him during the year.

One day while Rick was driving in Hyannis, he noticed workmen tearing down a building. A 275-gallon oil tank was lying next to a pile of debris from the building.

"Problem solved," Rick thought. "I can make that into a barbeque for my party." He made arrangements to have the tank picked up, but there was a problem. The tank still had heating oil in it. Rick found several ten-gallon containers. He had the oil pumped out of the tank and into the containers and then added the oil to his home oil tank—the oil warmed his home nicely for some time.

After the tank was emptied and cleaned, he had it cut and hinges installed on each side to make the tank easier to open. Several holes were drilled into a one-inch pipe which was installed inside the tank so that the barbeque could be gas fed. A thermometer was installed to keep track of the temperature. Hoses were used to connect the gas tank to the burner. The outside of the tank was painted with special black paint and then personalized with silver initials "RJD." The grill is kept on a flat-bottom trailer so it can easily be rolled to any location in the yard.

The first year the homemade grill was used there was almost a disaster. Bob left the pig unattended for too long and, when he lifted the lid to check it, the pig was on fire! But quick thinking Rick and Bob got the garden hose and doused the flames. Fortunately, no harm was done. Only the thick skin had burned. Underneath the burnt skin the pig meat was tender, juicy, and delicious.

During pig roast time, Rick is happiest. He loves people and loves doing for others. He has an ability to smile, be positive and compliment individuals. His radiant human spirit is contagious. He is always willing to help anyone and asks nothing in return. The more he interacts the happier he is. When my neighbor back in Worcester attended the party for the first time she said, "I often thought about Rick and felt sorry to see him in a wheelchair, but now that I know how happy his life is, I don't feel that way anymore." He greets every guest with a big smile; you don't see the wheelchair at all when you are in his presence.

The day before the pig roast his entire family arrives with sleeves rolled up and raring to go. Rick scoots around in his electric wheelchair like a movie director, telling all of us what to do and where to put things. If any question comes up, the answer is, "Ask Rick."

Guests start arriving at four o'clock. Rick greets them and directs them to have a cold drink. A bar is set up close to the deck, with soft drinks packed in ice, as well as kegs of beer and bottles of wine. Hors d'oeuvres are plentiful. The desserts are set up on the open dining room table that is covered with a linen tablecloth. In the center is a bouquet of fresh flowers. Everything imaginable is brought to the dessert table from chocolate chip cookies to tortes of all kinds. The other foods, consisting of various salads, vegetables and specialty dishes are placed on a long picnic table near the barbeque grill. One guest customarily brings 400 clam casinos ready to be topped with bacon and baked. As soon as they are taken out of the oven, like a vacuum, they disappear. My husband starts the gas grill and places hot dogs, chicken, hamburgers and sausage on it. The pig is started early in the morning. It takes all day to cook and uses two tanks of gas. The children are always curious about the progress of the cooking pig. They must take a peek. Bob is there to watch over it carefully. The majority of the guests finally arrive and the last food served is the roasted pig. There is always someone there who will put an apple in its mouth and sunglasses on its eyes. The cooked pig is carefully transferred from the grill to a huge table that is covered with aluminum foil. One guest who has some knowledge about carving does a super job slicing the pork. The pig roast is a joyous occasion for everyone.

Very few guests remain seated at tables. They circle around to talk to one another with plates of food and drinks in hand, and, all are laughing and joking. Most of the guests know one another although often times they have not seen each other since the last pig roast. Therefore many are catching up on news. The band starts playing at seven o'clock. The leader of the band will walk through the aisles between tables where the guests are eating, and place the microphone in front of several of the guests so they can sing along. This creates some loud laughter because most of the time the notes are very flat. The deck is large enough to stimulate dancing feet to do some fancy dance steps. Rick has the biggest smile on his handsome face, and looking at his expression would make anyone feel exhilarated.

The party continues until the wee hours of the morning. The guests eat and drink all the while. They are a very respectful crowd and no one becomes troublesome. Some of the guests, for safety reasons, pitch tents in the spacious front yard and stay the remainder of the night.

The next morning, it's clean up time. Once again, Rick's family and some friends arrive to organize, pack, and clean things for the next year's party. Bob is in charge of cleaning the barbeque grill where the pig was cooked. It takes a lot of cleaning solution and elbow grease to scrub the grill clean. After the grill is cleaned and dried, Bob applies a thin coat of oil to the interior to prevent rusting. The entire cleaning process takes several hours. The rented tables and chairs are loaded in a station wagon and returned. All unused supplies are boxed and stored again in the basement for the next year's pig roast.

A week later, all the scratch tickets are scratched. The jackpot from the tickets sometimes just covers the cost of the paper supplies. The guests get a big kick out of bringing the tickets, and Rick feels it is a way to make the party a little different and exciting. What's not to love about this annual party!

CHAPTER SEVENTEEN

THE AWARD

The phone rang in Rick's office on a bright sunny morning in the spring of 1999. Diana was there to take the call. A male voice on the other end of the line wanted to speak to Rick. The person calling was Joe Lane, the athletic director of St. John's High School in Shrewsbury, and Rick had not the faintest notion of why Joe would call. They chatted briefly but soon Joe got to the point. He told Rick that he had been selected to receive the prestigious Bruce S. Kopka Memorial Award presented for courage, perseverance and character.

Each year the school selects outstanding individuals for this award. The Kopka Award was formed in cooperation with the Kopka family and the school to keep the spirit of Bruce alive. Bruce played four years of varsity football and earned a reputation as a dedicated, hard-nosed football player. He was voted the team's best defensive player for three consecutive years and was elected captain in his senior year. Shortly after his graduation, he was diagnosed as having lupus. Through it all he completed his college education and became gainfully employed with the United States Postal Service. In late 1985 Bruce suffered a setback in his battle against lupus. This once promising athlete finally fell to this deadly disease in January 1986. He embodied the spirit which the Kopka Award seeks to memorialize.

It is our family tradition to celebrate Thanksgiving Day on Cape Cod. The atmosphere on the Cape is quaint and quiet at that time of year. The streets are not busy or crowded and shopping is not a hassle. Our family drives down from Worcester for the annual feast. My daughter's mother-in-law who lives five miles away from our Cape home prepares the traditional turkey dinner with all the trimmings. The day after Thanksgiving we eat a traditional Italian meal of lasagna, antipasto, fried eggplant, ice cream and any left over pumpkin, apple and mincemeat pies at our Dennis home. I serve a group of twelve. It is certainly an eating weekend.

But in 1999, the year Joe Lane called, we did not spend the entire Thanksgiving weekend on the Cape. Instead, on Saturday, we attended a dinner at beautiful Wachusett Country Club, a restaurant situated on a hill with a panoramic view of the city at night and a plush golf course during the day. The award from St. John's High was given to Rick twenty-five years after his high school graduation. Later he was to receive other awards but none meant so much as this one.

For the occasion, Rick was dressed in a white shirt, tie and sport jacket, attire he is not comfortable wearing. He feels his arm movements are restricted. Therefore he had his friend Jim Nally drive the van to West Boylston for the affair. Julie came with them.

When we arrived at the restaurant, we were graciously escorted to a VIP room where we were served cocktails and hors d'oeuvres. The room was filled with all those who were to receive awards as well as their families. Next we went to our table for ten which included our family and some special friends. It was located close to the head table where Rick sat. All of a sudden, realizing he had to address 250 people, my mature confident son had regressed to a ten-year-old who needed our constant laughing reassurance to calm him.

I tried to soothe him by saying, "You'll be fine but just don't speak too fast."

"O.K. Mom, I'll start my speech by saying my mother told me not to speak too fast," Rick replied.

When Joe Lane, acting as master of ceremonies, called upon Rick to accept his award Rick handled himself well. He spoke eloquently, clearly and without notes. His speech was divided into three parts. First he expressed thanks to the staff for putting up with him when he was at St John's. Second, he thanked God for giving him the patience he never knew he had and finally thanked his family and friends for their support. After his speech he received a very impressive standing ovation. And every member of our group and many of the other attendees had to wipe their eyes.

After all the awards were presented, Joe Lane came to Rick to congratulate him and praise him for a job well done. Joe noted that Rick was the only recipient who had not used notes. He had spoken from his heart. Joe told Rick that he was inspired by his courage, determination and success. And so, the St. John's family welcomed Richard J. D'agostino into a select group of young men as that year's Kopka Memorial Award Recipient. He was given a trophy—a beautiful clock, which he treasures.

CHAPTER EIGHTEEN

A TRIBUTE TO RICK

by Penny Kiefer

Meeting Rick back in the mid 1980s was a blessing—in too many ways to count. Little did I know how this handsome and gentle soul would influence the person whom I have become today.

Back at our initial meeting I saw something in his eyes I never really had seen before. The look was compelling, and I couldn't put my finger on it for a while, but eventually I learned what it was. Gratefulness, pure and simple. Rick was a great human being. I can still remember walking away from his wheelchair as he soaked up rays of sunshine and then turning to look back at him as I made a mental note to see him again, even if it was only for a dose of the cheerfulness which that magnanimous smile radiated. As I glanced back, the sunlight caught on the stainless steel of his chair and shot a bright white glow my way if only for a moment.

I went in the computer lab to see Rick whenever I needed a genuine lift to my spirit. He was more positive in assessing life's problems than anyone I knew with the use of all their limbs. He was truly inspirational. I wanted to seek and find the same connectedness to life that Rick exuded. Through him I understood that to seek contentedness one needed to probe no further than oneself. I saw Rick's incredible self-confidence was not contained in or gleamed in the eyes of the onlooker, but from inside himself. I am sure that, to this very day, he has no idea that he inadvertently taught me one of the most important lessons of my life.

I had known Rick for a few years when I was 28 years old. I suffered a serious infection that almost claimed my life, which left me with a scarred body that needed to be rehabbed into functionality again. After being in the hospital for a month and a half, I found myself grateful to be released back into the life I had known before I became ill. The world looked like an exciting beautiful place again. I couldn't wait to explore the great depths of it. It was like a new place, and I was grateful if only for a few days before I allowed reality to bear down on me to push that gratefulness aside.

It took a while for me to be willing to leave my house on those crutches I had become so adept at using. I had never experienced a physical disability before, and having been previously athletic, I found myself feeling crushed by people staring at my disfigured leg. One day I went to the college to see all the professors who I had not seen since I was hospitalized. While I was there, I went to see Rick. He wasn't in the computer lab the first two times I stopped by. I felt a flood of relief when I saw him the third time I stopped by. I wanted to cry, in self-pity, but I was conscious of the fact that Rick would accept me exactly as I was, horribly disfiguring scars and all. I bit my lip so as not to let the dam holding back my tears break and smiled as I saw Rick's face. I was so tall and skinny from being so seriously ill, and, felt haggard from the lack of sympathy I had read as rejection. In reality, I didn't need anyone's sympathy, as I felt bad enough for myself. Rick looked up, smiled and said, "Hi doll." He motioned for me to kiss him on the cheek which I did, and, to my amazement, he never asked, maybe he never noticed, my predicament. He just chatted with me for a few minutes. Of course, being such a self-absorbed being at the time, I blurted out the whole story of what I had been through. It didn't seem to faze him at all. He smiled and said, "Oh, well, time to move on." For a moment I was indignant at his refusal to play my sympathy game, but it was difficult to stay provoked as I looked at him in his lowly wheelchair. I went home and I thought about that encounter for a long time. Big Lesson!

Later that same year I bought two dogs from him. I had always been a "dog person" and was aware of the level of loyalty and devotion a dog offered unconditionally to those who loved them. Rick would stop by and see the dogs as they grew. Not too often, just a few times a year. The dog, a great puppy named "Samantha" became a titled Rottweiler long before her mature adult dog status, would recognize the sound of Rick's wheelchair lift in his van and her eager anticipation to see her former owner (until 10 weeks old) would register in her total loss of composure. Sammy would pant, whine and struggle to contain herself and as his electric wheelchair approached, she would try to crawl right onto his lap. Her pleasure in seeing Rick was matched only by his joy in seeing her. As a dedicated dog person, I knew the implication of her action was a loyalty that knew no boundaries. Sammy was well aware of how truly special Rick was and is.

Likeable, kindhearted Rick, he takes advantage of his many talents and lays none to waste. Sometimes I would look at his unmoving legs as he explained this invention he had in his mind and marveled at them. His legs were always tanned and his feet were firmly planted on the footrests of his wheelchair. I would be amazed. Even in his chair he exuded confidence. He had the same "stance" which only a self-realized confident man would portray when standing on both feet. He had something else in those shining eyes as well, this gratefulness, that in my years of working with the public as a registered nurse I saw only on very old, contented folks who had a certain knowing about them. One doesn't see this knowing degree of self-assurance often in our rushed society.

I am grateful for the opportunity of knowing this gem, Rick. I am grateful to see the aura of self-confidence, love, and graciousness with an understanding for all sentient human beings. He is a diamond, for sure.

CHAPTER NINETEEN

THE BRIGHTER SIDE

Tears have dampened many pages of this book as it was being written, but they are dry now. The only tears I will shed will be with pride in my son's life. My heart has a hole in it that has grown smaller over the years, but will never disappear. It is there for the rest of my life. I thank God every day for seeing my son and I also thank the staff at the pool that saved him from drowning. He has brought much joy to our entire family during his challenging fifty years. These years have been quite a journey for Rick and for us.

A person must spend one full day with Rick—from the time he is removed from his bed in the morning until the evening when he is put to bed—to experience first-hand the physical and social barriers he is faced with every day of his life. His outer body is visibly broken but the inner is untouched. Rick views his life as being abundant with meaning and purpose. He broke his neck but it did not break him. His handicap enhanced his ability to help others. Without his suffering, the growth that he has achieved would not have been possible. It was his positive attitude and his faith throughout his life that helped him through this tragedy.

He still has to deal with problems that the rest of us don't face. But he is able to surmount those problems with patience, imagination, and fortitude. His life is not an easy one, but he does not complain.

When meeting him for the first time, it is normal for people to focus on his disability. Sitting in his wheelchair, Rick extends his right hand which is covered with a driving splint, to give the customary hand shake. Usually the newcomer lightly touches Rick's paralyzed finger in a desire not to cause him pain. The visitor perceives Rick as frail and is quite conscious of his disability.

But after a few minutes something wonderful takes place. The newcomer forgets about the wheelchair, and forgets that Rick is disabled and that in some ways he is far different from the rest of us.

Rick is poised, confident, optimistic, and upbeat. He does not look or act like someone who is a quadriplegic. He is full of life and energy. He is eager to meet people and to learn what makes them tick.

A friend of his told me, "Whenever I feel down I come to visit Rick. He makes me feel better." It is a common sentiment. It is his spirit that makes a difference. He is indomitable.

When Rick was in rehab, a therapist at Boston University Hospital for the spinal cord injured told me that the accident would not change my son's personality. Today, after more than three decades in his electric wheelchair, the therapist has been proven to be correct. Rick is the same as always—kind, compassionate, generous and sensible. I often go to him with a problem, because he always finds a solution.

As a toddler each time I took him with me to the bank and the teller would give him a lollipop, Rick would always ask for one for his brother. At the age of sixteen he was hired as a part-time gas attendant. He liked earning his own money. One Mother's Day, while I was asleep, he quietly assembled an exercise bicycle he had bought for my present. When I came into the kitchen, there was the assembled bicycle with a huge note: "Happy Mother's Day."

Rick has impacted many lives—not the least of which were the lives of women who became his friends. He was as helpful to them as they were to him. And Rick often helped them to overcome the obstacles in their lives, and to set and achieve their goals. He was always generous, emotionally and materially.

Rick loves restaurants, but only very good ones. To qualify, as one of Rick's choices, a restaurant must have linen table cloths and napkins, fresh flowers, real butter—not in a packet—and of course good food. Anytime we go out for dinner, we first consult Rick for an expert recommendation.

Rick is also a computer whiz. He can accomplish all sorts of feats on his machine from producing complex images to such tasks as creating his friend Angela's wedding invitations. There is often a strange computer in his living room since he is able to fix sick machines. Sometimes it takes several days but he always succeeds.

Rick enjoys digital photography and manipulating images on his computer. One time, when I was with him, he produced a picture of himself on the computer screen. The picture showed the ugly scar in the center of his throat from the tracheotomy he endured at the time of the accident. "Watch this," he said. After hitting a few keys the scar disappeared. As a computer illiterate, I was amazed.

Rick is a perfectionist and I must admit it can be annoying. He is apt to tell a person how to perform a certain task when the doer is perfectly capable of performing it on his own. His perfectionism causes him frustration which sometimes leads to a need for antacids.

My husband, Tony, spends three quarters of his time with Rick. He is Rick's hands and legs. He is completely devoted to him. Tony fixes every thing. He checks the wheelchair battery and tires and assembles the mock-ups for Rick's inventions. In more than thirty years Rick's wheelchairs have never been to a repair shop, except when one had to be welded together after being mangled in the van accident years ago. With Rick's technical mind and Tony's talented hands, repairs are completed. On many occasions the van's lift has broken. Rick has used a cell phone attached to his wheelchair and called Tony for help. In almost no time at all the repair would be made. We can only imagine the frustration of being stranded in the van, unable to get out.

Tony is also Rick's handyman around the house. He maintains the yard, fixes plumbing and carpentry problems and exhibits talent as a painter. I gave him the official title of "Shipping Clerk" because he ships packages and products which have been repaired back to the customers. Obviously Tony is busy, a good thing for a man in his mid-eighties. These responsibilities keep him alert, agile and happy to be useful.

For one full year, while Tony was working with Rick, he constantly complained of not feeling well. He felt achy and physically exhausted. After feeling this way too long he went to a doctor and was finally tested and found to have Lyme disease. We did some research and found a specialist in infectious disease that took such cases. Now we had to get an appointment with this busy doctor. This diagnosis disturbed Rick. He sat at his computer and painstakingly sent the doctor an e-mail that read:

Re: Need your help with Lyme Disease

Dear Dr. Donta:

My name is Rick D'Agostino and I was told you're a miracle worker when it comes to Lyme disease.

I'm writing regarding my Dad, he's 83 years old and my best friend. You see, I broke my neck when I was 17 (33 years ago) and my dad has been my hands ever since. He works with me almost every day.

For quite a while he has been feeling shitty, sleeps poorly, no energy, sore joints and so on. Everything equated with getting old be that he is a young 83.

You have to understand, he is a little Italian power house, strong as an ox, athletic, and normally can out work all of us. He looks like he is in his early 60s.

Right after Mother's Day I thought he had a small stroke or TIA. He said he slept great the night before and when he got up in the morning he could not read the newspaper. He could not focus or think straight.

We worked together that morning and I could tell he wasn't right. I made him go to the Emergency Room at Cape Cod Hospital and get some tests. CT scan, and blood work, turned out negative.

That night my mother and sister came down from Worcester and brought him back home. The next morning he went to UMass Medical for a complete battery of test, MRI, spinal tap and on and on.

They tested for Lyme Disease and it came back positive.

I am really hoping you can see him. I want him treated by someone who specializes in this disease and can aggressively treat him.

I know I can't have him around forever, but there are still plenty of good years left in him and I would like him to feel good, not shitty all the time.

Thanks for your time.

Sincerely,

*Rick D'Agostin*o

Almost immediately, the doctor himself called us for an appointment. My husband had a visit with him in Falmouth and continues to receive treatment. He is slowly beginning to feel better.

My elder son, Bob, is also devoted to his brother. As often as possible to get free time from his work, he spends two or three days with Rick. He prepares his specialty gourmet meals, and in front of the fire they discuss sports and the problems of the world or they sit quietly and enjoy the brotherly camaraderie.

Gina, his sister, helps him in a more practical way. As the mother of two teenagers who works full-time at the hospital, she does not have much free time. However, she helps by assembling electric bag emptiers for Rick to sell. All needed supplies are brought to her. She puts together the gadgets and ships them to the Cape for coming sales.

I spend roughly half of my time on the Cape, keeping Rick's books and doing other office chores. He saves special household chores for me to do. Although he has a cleaning woman, I help him sort out closets and drawers. Rick's perfectionism demands that his personal items be in a special order. I know Rick's favorite dishes, so I prepare several meals for him. Spaghetti sauce, chicken noodle soup and stews are his favorites. He is delighted to have them. "Beautiful" and "delicious" are his favorite words and he uses them often. He fully appreciates the help he receives.

Rick's accident has made us a close and supportive family. Each of us has a special field of expertise which benefits my son. My husband as a fire chief is concerned for his safety. My son Bob's physical education background helps keep Rick as physically fit as possible with proper diet and some exercise. My daughter focuses on a healthy heart. My nursing experience keeps me aware of any medication he is taking. We all contribute to his well-being. We work well together and draw strength from one another.

Denny is another very positive force in Rick's life. The entire routine takes approximate three or four hours. She then dashes off to her full time position as a Rehabilitation Nurse at Spaulding Rehab Center in Cambridge, Massachusetts. Denny and Rick are extremely close. She admires him and his accomplishments and in return he admires her strength and knowledge. We all give fervent thanks to Denny for her staunch, unwavering and compassionate care all these years. It is miraculous that Rick has never had a bedsore on his back in all the years he has spent confined to the wheelchair. This is thanks to Denny. She is an attractive mature woman in excellent physical condition. She works out to keep up her strength and controls her diet. She recently became a grandmother when her daughter gave birth to a son.

After Denny finishes her duties with Rick, he quickly goes into his office to start his day.

He reads his e-mail and answers telephone calls from all over the United States, Hawaii and Alaska. Later on, Rick will fasten his chest harness to get ready to enter his van to do some of his routine errands such as banking, dry cleaning, grocery shopping and so forth. He travels alone but relies on people to help him when he arrives at his destination. On his wheelchair he has attached a small box that contains his credentials and his wallet. The person is instructed by Rick to remove a certain amount from his wallet to complete the sale. He has never had any trouble with this arrangement. At lunchtime, he usually has soup with his Dad.

Rick plans dinner before Julie arrives home from work. Recently he presented Julie with a flawless diamond set in platinum. She was delighted. At the age of fifty he is finally settling down. We wish them good luck and much happiness. We must wait and see when a wedding date is planned.

Julie, Rick and Jessie have dinner together. Many times they have dinner delivered or go to a restaurant. In the evening they often watch a movie or just enjoy one another's company.

Rick loves people. He gets along with everyone. Many times friends riding by will drop in to chat with Rick. His house is always full of people. He is generous. A friend's daughter needed some capital to start a jewelry business and without hesitation, he gave her five thousand dollars. Another time, a friend ran out of cash while on vacation and he sent him two thousand dollars. I have no idea if they ever paid him back.

At Christmas time Rick contacts the Salvation Army to receive the name of a needy child. They give him the first name, sex, sizes and color preferences, and then he gets a complete outfit for the child. This is the "Dress a Living Doll" program. The donor selects a complete wardrobe for the child from top to bottom and inside and out with exception of shoes. It's fun for the donor and a grand Christmas gift for the child. Rick does all the shopping and I wrap each package with festive Christmas paper, then the boxes are loaded in his van to be distributed by the Salvation Army to the delight of a little child.

My husband and I went on a vacation to the beautiful island of Jamaica, while there I met a young girl from Cape Cod. We had a brief discussion. I was concerned about the accessibility of the island because Rick, Julie and Denny were to arrive the following week. As I spoke to the lovely young girl she mentioned she was a nurse and asked the name of my son. When I told her, her face showed great surprise. She had taken care of Rick for just two days, but had to request to be removed from the case. She was falling in love with her patient. She could not help but kiss him goodbye when she left. When I arrived home, I told Rick about her. He remembered the kiss but could not remember her name.

Like Barbara Streisand's song "People Who Need People Are the Luckiest People in the World" that's my son. He is lucky he will never be lonesome for there will always be someone to get him in and out of bed, lucky also to have his own beautiful home, lucky to have Julie and Jessica with him, lucky to have his loving and devoted family, lucky to be financially stable, and lucky to have his many loyal friends.

I hope that by telling my story, I will help other people who have faced tragic, life-changing experiences. It is a book about a family with a disabled child, and not about aches and pains and medicines but attitudes toward the disability. I have a favorite saying "The only disability is a bad attitude." Telling the life of my son has been a tremendously uplifting experience. This story that I have shared I hope will be a wellspring of inspiration. The journey has made me a stronger person and a more resilient, more confident woman than I ever was. I hope you will find something in this book of value to you in the course of the journey accomplished in a wheelchair.

The richness and fullness of Rick's life spring from the gifts he brings to other lives. His creativity has produced products that have enriched other disabled lives. His disability became a source of an inspiring future accomplished through courage, determination, patience and compassion. He inspired people he met to triumph over adversity and he will continue to do so everyday day of his life. Rick views his life as being abundant with meaning and purpose. He broke his neck but it didn't break him. His handicap enhanced his ability to help others. Without his suffering, the growth he has achieved would not have been possible. It's ability not disability that counts. He truly is an inspiration.

I have found deep meaning in what Paul says in his letter to the Romans: "For those who love God and are called in his plan, everything works for the good."

Do I wish that Rick had never been injured? Of course, But I know that as a result of our experience, we are all more loving, more giving, more mature, and more blessed than we could have thought possible.

I don't understand why some people suffer more than others and why Rick became a quadriplegic. But I know something now that I did not know before I wrote this book.

We prayed for a miracle, and we got one, and the miracle's name is Rick.

Gilda T. D'Agostino, one of nine children, is a retired registered nurse who received a bachelor's degree in Health Sciences and Psychology at the age of 74. She and her husband Tony have three children, Robert, Richard and Gina. Gilda divides her time between her Cape Cod and Worcester, Massachusetts homes.

All proceeds from this book will be donated to benefit research for the cure of spinal cord injuries.